The
Language
of Risk

SOME PAST VOLUMES IN THE
SAGE FOCUS EDITIONS

The Language of Risk

Conflicting Perspectives on Occupational Health

Edited by

Dorothy Nelkin

SAGE PUBLICATIONS Beverly Hills London New Delhi

Copyright © 1985 by Sage Publications, Inc.

For information address:

SAGE Publications, Inc.
275 South Beverly Drive
Beverly Hills, California 90212

SAGE Publications India Pvt. Ltd.
M-32 Market
Greater Kailash I
New Delhi 110 048 India

SAGE Publications Ltd
28 Banner Street
London EC1Y 8QE
England

Printed in the United States of America

Library of Congress Cataloging in Publication Data

Main entry under title:

The language of risk.

   (Sage focus edition ; v. 71)
   Includes bibliographies and index.
   1. Industrial hygiene—United States. 2. Industrial safety—United States. 3. Labor and laboring classes—United States—Attitudes. 4. Chemicals—Hygienic aspects.
I. Nelkin, Dorothy.
HD7654.L36   1985   363.1'1'0973   85-2211
ISBN 0-8039-2466-6
ISBN 0-8039-2467-4 (pbk.)

FIRST PRINTING

The
Language
of Risk

CONTENTS

PREFACE

The chapters included in this volume were written as part of a project on workers' perceptions of occupational risk. The authors of the chapters, all participants in this project, were struck by the diversity of issues and the range of actors involved in the arena of occupational health. Beyond the central role of labor and management, evaluating and managing workplace risks engages scientists, physicians, journalists, administrators, and policy analysts. Each group brings its own mode of thought and professional concerns to the varied problems of occupational health. By mapping this complex arena, we hope to contribute to an understanding of the conflicting values that perpetuate disputes over risk.

The chapters all gained from discussion among the authors during the course of the project. They were partly based on research supported by the National Science Foundation Program on Ethics and Values in Science and Technology, Grant ISP 8112920. The opinions and conclusions expressed are those of the authors and do not necessarily reflect the views of the National Science Foundation. I would also like to acknowledge the Russell Sage Foundation where, as a visiting scholar, I had the time to edit and compile the chapters.

Dorothy Nelkin
Ithaca, NY

INTRODUCTION: ANALYZING RISK

Dorothy Nelkin

In 1855, a British tourist, Charles Weld, was traveling on an American train when it began to shudder and shake. Panicked, he asked the conductor to stop the train, but to no avail. The train jumped the tracks and many of the cars were smashed. Yet, to Weld's amazement, his fellow passengers applauded the conductor's efforts to arrive on time. So consumed were they by the ideology of progress that they failed to recognize a near-fatal disaster.[1]

Clearly, attitudes have changed. Although the development of science and technology remained largely unquestioned during the period of rapid economic growth that followed World War II, faith in technological progress has since been tempered by growing awareness of risks. Technological improvements have caused grave environmental problems. Pesticides, essential to food production, also are carcinogens. Innovative industrial processes have threatened and harmed workers' health. We are deluged with warnings about "invisible hazards": PCBs, freon, radiation, dioxin, and a bewildering array of chemicals. We are in constant contact with such products in our homes and at our work.

Public concern about risk is expressed in frequent controversies over technological decisions.[2] Thousands of people have participated in protests against nuclear power, converging at reactor sites to prevent construction of power plants that they believe will damage the environment and pose risks to public health. Similarly, controversies have delayed decisions about the disposal of toxic wastes. While most risk disputes have revolved around environmental issues, they are increasingly coming to focus on the workplace—on the problems of occupational health. This is the context in which this book explores the politics of risk.

Public concern over both environmental and occupational risk is reflected in litigation, legislation, and regulation. Disputes frequently are brought to court as individuals seek compensation for health problems resulting from exposure to toxic substances. They reach the legislatures and regulatory agencies as activists seek to influence the standards regulating the use of chemicals and to assure the implementation of these standards. They reach the press as risk events frequently are reported as front page news.

Risk disputes are complicated, involving political choices as well as technical evaluations of hazards. Evaluating risk requires judgments in the face of uncertainty and scientific disagreement. What constitutes significant and meaningful evidence? Whose judgment is to be considered in evaluating the severity and acceptability of risk? What rules of evidence should guide legal and policy decisions? Controlling risk involves questions of equity and political responsibility. What are the appropriate roles and limits of government in regulating industrial practices? Who should be involved in decisions about risk? How should workers, affected communities, and the general public be informed? These are deeply divisive questions that characterize the increasingly heated debates over the risks assumed by millions of people who work with chemicals and chemical products.

Chemical products are indispensable to the modern economy. They provide not only the raw materials for fundamental industrial processes but also the components of a huge number of intermediate products (organic chemicals, pesticides, plastics, and solvents) and an unprecedented number of consumer goods (cosmetics, records, paint, and plastic bags). The proliferation of chemicals—about 1000 new chemicals reach the market each year—has brought advances in medicine and sanitation. Chemicals have helped to provide durable clothing, cheaper food, and better housing. They have opened new markets and provided employment. But these achievements are not without risk, especially to the health of the growing number of people exposed to toxic chemicals in their daily work.

The stakes in defining, measuring, and evaluating the risks of working with chemicals are high, and many different groups are involved. Disputes over occupational risk obviously divide labor and management, the principal adversaries in the workplace. Their approaches to risk reflect their economic interests, for defining risks can impose costs, allocating responsibility for cleaning up a workplace or liability for compensating those who suffer health problems. In a sense, then, labor and management are playing out their traditional roles, casting this new issue into the familiar mold that has been shaped by long-standing adversarial relationships. But disputes over risk also engage and polarize a variety of other groups: scientists, company doctors, lawyers, agency administrators, journalists, and policy experts. Their assumptions and beliefs about risk reflect more than economic stakes; professional ideologies, bureaucratic routines, career pressures, and political predilections all influence their role in risk disputes. These groups approach disputed issues with sets of assumptions, modes of analysis, ideological frameworks that shape their definitions of the problem, filter their perceptions, guide their judgments, and influence their responses.

The essays in this volume are directed at clarifying the diverse and often conflicting modes of thought that enter the discourse and affect public policies concerning occupational health. They go beyond the usual interest group polarization to

examine the many interacting and competing points of view
that have been activated by controversies over risk and regulation in the workplace. They approach the perspectives and
political strategies of different actors primarily by analyzing
the discourse of risk disputes. To put this approach in context,
let us first briefly review the main thrust of research in the field
of risk analysis as it has evolved over the past few decades.

APPROACHING THE PROBLEM OF RISK

Systematic efforts to estimate and evaluate the risks inherent
in different technologies first developed in response to growing
public concern about nuclear power in the late 1960s. Subsequently, the field of risk analysis has become a veritable industry, engaging professionals versed in "objective" methodologies: engineers, systems analysts, economists, psychologists,
anthropologists, and sociologists. Seeking a "rational" means
to make decisions about hazardous technologies, most risk
analysts have sought to establish a quantitative basis by which
to compare the risks from different technological choices, to
calculate their relative costs and benefits, and to assess their
public acceptability. Encouraged by legislation requiring that
the risks of technological choices be systematically weighed
against their social benefits, they have developed a number of
distinct approaches.

Some analytic approaches to risk are based on engineering
and economic models, including forecasting and systems analysis techniques.[3] Based on measures of mortality and morbid-
ity, they seek to calculate in an objective manner the probabili-
ties of a hazardous event, to identify the consequences for
human health, and to estimate the likelihood of these consequences. However, the fundamental uncertainties about the
nature and extent of the risks inherent in many technological
choices often defy systematic analysis. Sometimes the efforts to

quantify risks and benefits have simply masked real uncertainties. Often the estimation of risk has ignored the nonquantifiable, fragile values—the emotional distress or the disruption of social relationships—that are associated with technological risks. Generally, the efforts to calculate the risks and benefits of technology have failed to predict the political and social acceptability of risk. This difficulty in predicting public attitudes and behavior in response to potentially hazardous technologies has encouraged research on the factors that enter subjective perceptions of risk.

Human responses to risk are filled with contradictions. Countless aphorisms warn us about risk, but their directions are not clear: "Look before you leap" conveys a different message than "he who hesitates is lost." Our behavior in the face of risk also is inconsistent. In our role as citizens we seek increased government protection (by supporting seat-belt legislation, for example), whereas in our role as consumers we often fail to comply. We are concerned about chemicals, yet we smoke. Some technologies (e.g., nuclear power) evoke more fear than others (e.g., coal), although this may have little to do with the actual extent of risk. Public perceptions of risk often differ from the judgments of experts. Yet biases enter the judgments of experts as well. Thus, understanding the acceptability of risk must begin with an analysis of attitudes and how they are shaped.

Psychologists employ laboratory experiments, gaming situations, and survey techniques in order to understand the sources of risk perception. For example, an important group of studies organized by Paul Slovic and other psychologists in the field of decision theory has described the characteristics of different kinds of risk that seem to influence judgments about their acceptability.[4] They suggest that risks that are involuntary, uncertain, unfamiliar, and potentially catastrophic (for example, the invisible and invidious risks of radiation or chemical pollution) are most difficult for people to accept. Familiar and voluntary activities, such as smoking, driving, or skiing, may be more dangerous, yet are more easily accepted. Other factors, such as a person's distance from the source of risk and the imaginability of certain consequences, may enter individual evaluations.

This line of inquiry aims to arrive at a quantitative determination of risk acceptance. However, the results have been limited by the assumption that perceptions depend mainly on the characteristics of the risk itself. Although the studies consider aggregate attitudes toward different types of risk situations, they do not take into consideration the subjective perceptions that are associated with membership in a social class or involvement in a social milieu. They fail to account for variations in the perception of similar risks in different social, cultural, or institutional contexts, and among different social groups. Why, indeed, did Charles Weld perceive the risks of a railway accident so differently from the Americans on the train?

These social dimensions of risk perception have attracted the interest of anthropologists and sociologists, who explicitly argue that risk perception is a social or cultural concept. Concerns about risk may depend less on the nature of the danger than on the observer's political and cultural biases. It is the social system, the world view, the ideological premises of a group or a society that shapes perceptions of risk. According to anthropologist Mary Douglas, a leading proponent of this view, beliefs about risk are embedded in a complex system of beliefs and values.[5] Judgments about risk are a social comment. The concepts of accountability, responsibility, and liability that pervade debates about risk are in effect political statements expressing points of tension and value conflicts in a given society.

Sociologists argue that risk perception also can reflect institutional arrangements, social situations, and political relationships. Blue-collar workers are likely to see risks differently than their supervisors. Scientists view dangers in the laboratory through different lenses than technicians. Social scientists look to the social setting in which people experience risk as a source of their attitudes and a guide to their responses.[6] They assume that debates about risk reflect concerns about economic, political, and social arrangements.

Still another line of inquiry, favored by lawyers and policy analysts, describes the nature of decisions concerning the control and regulation of risk. Concerned with managing risk so as to get on with the technological enterprise, these studies focus on the policies and institutions through which controls are implemented. They include studies of the formal and informal decision-making process, the legal and legislative institutions of control, the setting of standards, and the ways of implementing regulations. Many of these analysts examine the effect of interventionist policies, such as the banning of certain products, the restrictions on advertising, and the provision of public information.[7] Others focus on the cost of controlling risk—"the risk of risk decisions"—in terms of dollars spent on reducing hazards and productivity delays.[8] A related literature explores models of decision making that would reduce conflict in the area of risk and optimize the possibilities of legitimate decisions under conditions of uncertainty.[9] The point of these studies usually is to discover the relative effectiveness of various managerial and decision strategies and to assess their impact on technological innovation.

A CONFLICT APPROACH

The chapters in this volume follow the anthropological and sociological approaches to risk in assuming that the interests and biases of different groups and the social situation in which they are involved influence their perceptions of risk and their strategies of management and control. The authors concede that, within the limits imposed by technical uncertainty, it is useful to measure risks in terms of actual physical hazards and the physiological consequences of exposure. But they also recognize that evaluation and, more especially, the management and regulation of risk also involve perceptions and priorities that are shaped by economic, political, and ideological concerns. And they assume that defining and managing risk is fundamentally controversial—that risk assessment divides groups with competing interests and conflicting social outlooks. Indeed, a "Rashomon" syndrome pervades disputes over risk as various groups define the issues in ways that reflect their values, their visions, and their views.

At one level of risk disputes, all parties may subscribe to the same values; all value the importance of health. But as one probes beneath the surface systematic differences emerge. Is a problem of risk to be defined primarily as a technical matter of measurement and etiology? As a bureaucratic controversy over regulatory mechanisms and jurisdictions? As an economic question of measuring costs and benefits? As a political issue touching on consumer control? Or as a moral issue regarding the value of life?

Conflicting values in risk disputes assume special importance because of the uncertainty of technical knowledge. Some uncertainties persist because scientific information simply is not available. This is especially true in the case of the risk from toxic chemicals. According to the Environmental Protection Agency, of the 63,000 chemicals in commercial use today, only 10% have been adequately tested for health and safety. Of 350 chemicals that are suspected carcinogens, only 60 have been evaluated through epidemiological studies. An exhaustive study by the National Academy of Sciences in March of 1984 found that adequate information on potential health hazards exists for only 18% of 1,815 pharmaceutical products, 10% of 3,350 pesticide ingredients, 5% of 8,627 food additives, and 2% of 3,410 cosmetic ingredients.

Neither epidemiological nor laboratory studies can identify all the substances that may cause cancer, neurological problems, or genetic defects. Because of the limited possibilities for human experimentation, most laboratory studies testing the effects of chemicals must employ animals as research subjects, and their relevance to assessing human susceptibility remains in dispute. Although the health risks of exposure to some chemicals—such as asbestos, vinyl chloride, and benzene— have been clearly documented, the effects of many other substances are unknown.

Even for intensively studied substances, the relationship between risk and exposure often remains unclear. Scientific judgments about the effect of toxic substances on individual health are constrained by inadequate evidence, relatively primitive diagnostic techniques, and limited understanding of the mechanisms by which hazards may affect human health and the environment. The cumulative and synergistic effects of multiple exposures to combinations of substances are poorly documented. Moreover, chemicals may affect different people in different ways. It is especially difficult to draw causal associations between exposure to chemical substances and long-term health effects; for if exposure to toxic substances causes cancer, the symptoms may not become evident for many years.

Such scientific uncertainties allow for a wide range of evaluations and interpretations of risk. For example, estimates of the proportion of cancers that are thought to be directly related to industrial exposure vary from 5% to 20%.[10] With few standards to guide analysis, it hardly is surprising that specialists assessing risk arrive at divergent conclusions about the relative danger of particular hazards and the need for controls. Technical uncertainties influence the judgments of management and labor as they negotiate contracts concerning worker health, doctors as they diagnose medical problems, journalists as they write about occupational health, and policy makers as they struggle to establish regulatory standards. Conflict prevails over the significance of risk, the adequacy of evidence, the methodologies for evaluating and measuring risk, the severity of health effects, the appropriate standards to regulate industrial practice, and even the communication of risk information.

Philosopher Stephen Toulmin has suggested that "men who accept different paradigms have really no common theoretical terms in which to discuss their problems fruitfully. They will not even have the same problems."[11] This often is the case in disputes over occupational health. Thus, in dealing with the diverse dimensions of risk disputes, each of the chapters in this volume suggests how participants approach the issue through their own lenses, or what sociologists sometimes call a "frame." A frame is a set of assumptions that is axiomatic, unassailable, and subject to neither review nor verification. Martin Rein suggests that "a frame provides a vision in a world of doubt.... It grounds our interests and permits us to integrate facts and values."[12] Similarly, Todd Gitlin defines frames as "the principles of selection, emphasis and presentation that routinely organize discourse."[13] In effect, the facts to which we attend depend on the construction we impose on events.

Frames are grounded in cultural, institutional, or situational factors. They are expressed in language and in patterns of reasoning. We shall see in this volume how different groups describe risks and define solutions in diverse ways. Workers, managers, physicians, journalists, and scientists are involved. Some talk of cost-effective solutions, of efficiency; others use the language of "rights," emphasizing moral issues and questions of social responsibility, justice, and obligation. Some evaluate risk in statistical terms; others talk of "victims," or "real people." Some define risk as a problem that requires expert solutions; others seek more participatory controls.

The language used by different groups to describe risk and to prescribe solutions is judgmental. The terms employed frame an event; the metaphors and images used to describe a situation can point the finger of blame and imply responsibility for remedial action. Some words imply disorder or chaos, others certainty and scientific precision. Selective use of labels can trivialize an event or render it important; marginalize some groups, empower others; define an issue as a problem or reduce it to a routine. Is the discovery of PCBs a "disaster" or an "incident?" Are certain chemicals "doomsday products" or "potential risks?" Are risks unavoidable ("chemicals are a fact of life") or a result of deliberate choice? Is fear of risk a "phobia" or a realistic concern?

The choice of language, a reflection of values, also is strategic, for language carries implications for the formulation of policy. For example, if the problems of risk are defined in terms of insufficient technical evidence, this implies that "risk assessment," with all its connotations of objectivity and neutrality, is the appropriate approach to regulation, and that regulation is properly the province of expertise. If the problems are defined in the social or moral context of responsibility and social justice, this calls for more political approaches to public policy. In this way, the discourse frames the policy agenda.[14]

Conceptualizing the problems of risk in terms of conflicting values, the authors of the chapters in this volume explore the descriptions and definitions of occupational risk that emerge from different social and institutional contexts. By examining the discourse of the different actors in risk disputes they seek insight into the diverse modes of thought that shape the definition of problems, the allocation of responsibility, and the acceptability of policy solutions. They also examine the implications of these values for policy choices.

The first essay, by Stephen Hilgartner, explores the political language used by labor and management as they struggle to control the definition of the occupational health problem and thereby structure the policy agenda. Hilgartner highlights how underlying economic interests and competing visions of social justice are expressed in the discourse on occupational health and how the language of risk itself becomes an arena of political conflict.

The distribution of information about potential hazards is one of the most contentious issues in risk disputes. The central and controversial role of information in the management of risk is expressed in disputes over the labeling of chemicals, the terms of "right-to-know" legislation, the content of information to be provided to workers, and the means to implement their right to know. Michael S. Brown examines these contentious issues by comparing conflicting views about the communication of risk information in the workplace.

The media play a significant role in the discourse on risk. News reports often are the only means through which the general public becomes informed about occupational hazards. Journalists thus are key actors in risk disputes. Through their selection and construction of news about risk they help to shape public attitudes and define the policy agenda. Chris Anne Raymond compares the coverage of occupational risks and the language used to describe risk in two types of media: the mainline and advocacy presses. She suggests the role of different ideological biases in structuring the amount of news coverage and the images of risk that reach the public through the media.

Among the more controversial actors in disputes over occupational risk is the company doctor. Dorothy Nelkin examines the conflicting perspectives on the ethical integrity of this profession., While workers are extraordinarily mistrustful of corporate medical programs, professional assumptions about the scientific objectivity of medicine inhibit physicians' recognition of the problem of dual loyalty. Nelkin describes how the company doctor's adjudicatory responsibility to determine workers' eligibility for compensation or fitness to work perpetuates the tensions between doctors and their patients within the context of the firm.

Risk disputes inevitably come to focus on the administrative decisions of regulatory agencies. These decisions are guided by complex and often contradictory approaches that are based on both legalistic concepts and bureaucratic biases. Sheila Jasanoff examines how the language, the concepts, and the procedural rules adopted by regulatory agencies emerge from the clash between the legal and bureaucratic cultures. She shows how the dominance of the legal culture in agency decision making in the United States obstructs the effectiveness of administrative efforts to assess and regulate occupational risks.

Policy approaches to risk also are subject to different modes of thought. Some analysts follow the economic assumptions of cost-benefit analysis, others argue from concepts of justice and moral rights. Some appeal to our moral intuition, others to our sense of efficiency and order. Mark Sagoff compares and analyzes the philosophical grounds and policy implications of these contrasting approaches to risk. Informed by philosophical rather than sociological assumptions, his chapter provides an interesting contrast to the others. For Sagoff concludes that the two approaches in fact support each other; that consensus, not conflict, prevails.

The chapters as a whole map out the vested interests, philosophical assumptions, professional biases, and political ideologies that enter the definition, assessment, and management of risk. They shed light on the social, political, and economic influences that select particular risks for public attention and define them in specific ways. They illuminate the values that perpetuate disputes over risk and obstruct their resolution. Finally, they suggest the ways in which such disputes have come to symbolize the larger social divisions, philosophical differences, and political tensions within American society.

NOTES

1. From John Klasson, *Civilizing the Machine* (New York: Grossman, 1976). p. 48.

2. For case studies of such disputes, see Dorothy Nelkin, *Controversy: Politics of Technical Decisions* (Beverly Hills: Sage Publications, 1984).

3. See William Rowe, *An Anatomy of Risk* (New York: Riley, 1979). For a comprehensive bibliography on the field of risk analysis, see Vincent Covello and Mark Abernathy, "Risk Analysis and Technological Hazards: A Policy Related Bibliography," in *Technological Risk Assessment,* eds. C. Whipple et al. (The Netherlands: Sijthoff and Nordhoff, 1983).

4. Baruch Fischoff et al., *Acceptable Risk* (New York: Cambridge University Press, 1981).

5. Mary Douglas and Aaron Wildavsky, *Risk and Culture* (Berkeley: University of California Press, 1982). See also Steve Rayner, "Disagreeing About Risk," in *Risk Analysis, Institutions and Public Policy*, ed. S. G. Hadley (Port Washington, NY: Associated Faculty Press, 1984).

6. Dorothy Nelkin and Michael S. Brown, *Workers at Risk* (Chicago: University of Chicago Press, 1984).

7. See G. Majone, "Standard Setting and a Theory of Institutional Choice," *Policy and Politics* 5 (1977); and R. W. Kates and C. Hohenemser, eds., *Technological Hazard Management* (Cambridge, MA: Oelgeshlagger, Gunn & Hain, 1981).

8. Chauncey Starr and C. Whipple, "The Risk of Risk Decisions," *Science*, 6 June 1980, pp. 1114ff., R. C. Crandall, "Curbing the Cost of Social Regulation," *Brookings Bulletin* 15 (1977): 1-15.

9. See essays in R. C. Schwartz and W. A. Albers, eds., *How Safe is Safe Enough* (New York: Plenum Press, 1980); A. Tversky and D. Kahnemann, "Judgment Under Uncertainty," *Science* 185, (1974): 1124-1131.

10. For discussion of the technical uncertainties involved in diagnosing occupational sources of cancer, see Devra Lee Davis et al., "Estimating Cancer Causes: Problems in Methodology, Production and Trends," in *Banbury Report 9: Quantification of Occupational Cancer* (New York: Cold Springs Harbor Laboratory, 1981).

11. Stephen Toulmin, *Foresight and Understanding* (New York: Harper & Row, 1961), p. 57.

12. Martin Rein, "Value Critical Policy Analysis," in *Ethics, the Social Sciences and Policy Analysis*, eds. D. Callahan and B. Jennings (New York: Plenum Press, 1983), pp. 83-111.

13. Todd Gitlin, *The Whole World Is Watching* (Berkeley: University of California Press, 1980).

14. The theoretical basis for analyzing discourse as a means to conceptualize values and political strategies is laid out in Murray Edelman, *Political Language* (New York: Academic Press, 1977); George Lakoff and Mark Johnson, *Metaphors We Live By* (Chicago: University of Chicago Press, 1980).

1

THE POLITICAL LANGUAGE OF RISK: DEFINING OCCUPATIONAL HEALTH

Stephen Hilgartner

In our culture we view problems as puzzles, presuming that they have solutions. Once a "problem" is defined, possible "solutions" are considered. As action flows from the definition, the way a problem is framed has an important bearing on what is or is not done about it. Thus, defining social problems often becomes the center of fierce ideological battles. Which (of the many available problems) do we construe as requiring societal action? Which are not being addressed adequately by existing institutions and policy? Which (or whose) problems belong on the political agenda? In what terms are they framed? What metaphors and images do we use to understand and explain them? And what are the political and social implications of the metaphors we use?

This chapter examines the ways in which different interest groups use language to present their views about occupational health. It examines the political discourse in this controversy, comparing the ideologies, beliefs, and language used by industry and labor advocates, and exploring the ways in which these interest groups use language to frame issues and thereby influence policy.[1]

Language is a political tool, employed by interest groups to gain tactical advantage. Interest groups label their opponents. They define and redefine problems. They struggle to impose their definitions. They employ euphemism or vagueness to obscure issues. They conceal problematic judgments behind words of certitude. They use metaphor and imagery to express their ideologies, to dramatize issues, and to evoke support.

Murray Edelman argues that political language evokes and reinforces stock explanations for social problems. These explanations—or political myths—supply preset formulas for interpreting social conditions and events. A culture's political myths often are contradictory, providing conflicting explanations for the same situations. These opposing myths "depend upon unprovable premises about society and the individual."[2] and they provide the basis for a variety of political postures. This pattern clearly applies to the discourse about occupational health, in which the actors in risk disputes select different myths to interpret events and justify their actions.

Metaphors are important in evoking and expressing political myths. In *Metaphors We Live By*, George Lakoff and Mark Johnson show that, to a large extent, the conceptual system through which we view the world is based on metaphor.[3] Rather than a mere rhetorical flourish or turn of phrase, metaphor is basic to language, to our understanding of many concepts, and to our definitions of social problems. Thus, the choice of metaphor has political implications. In public discourse a metaphor can become a rallying point, a means of mobilizing public support.[4]

In examining the controversy about occupational health, this chapter analyzes the metaphors and political myths used by competing interest groups. The controversy is marked by divisions between the two main interest groups: industry advocates (e.g., company officials, trade associations, and business publications) and labor advocates (e.g., labor unions and advocacy organizations, such as Ralph Nader's Health Research Group). Industry and labor advocates disagree about the scope of the occupational health problem, the severity of chemical risks, the effectiveness of current efforts to protect workers, and the economic hazards of government regulation. But at a deeper level, the controversy reflects the long-standing, fundamental conflicts between management and workers. Thus, as the "new" issue of occupational health is discussed and debated, it becomes another arena for traditional adversarial workplace politics.

Inadequate scientific knowledge about chemical risks amplifies these basic conflicts, and disagreements are further compounded by uncertainty about the economic risks of government regulation.[5] Estimates of the costs and benefits of complying with Occupational Safety and Health Administration (OSHA) standards often differ substantially, and assessments of the long-term impact of regulation on the health of the economy are in even greater dispute.[6] Thus, depending on their interests, values, and philosophical outlooks, different people come up with dramatically different assessments of risks.

Industry and labor advocates hold strikingly different attitudes about a number of questions crucial to the controversy. How serious are workplace health risks? How threatening are the economic risks of regulations? Should government control of workplace practices be viewed as a form of repression or as protection of the citizenry? What imperatives should guide policy decisions: economic or moral ones? Are social relations marked by a confluence or a conflict of interests? The political discourse of industry and labor advocates clearly expresses these differing notions of risk, of control in the workplace, of the imperatives that should guide action, and of consensus and conflict in society.

In examining the political discourse, this chapter mainly uses business and labor publications and Congressional hearings as source material. It is important to note that the views of industry advocates are more fully represented in public discourse than those of labor. Examples of the industry position are easier to find and tend to appear in publications such as *Business Week* and *Fortune*, which reach wide audiences. In contrast, the labor view appears mostly in limited-circulation newsletters.

ON HEALTH RISKS

INDUSTRY ADVOCATES

Industry advocates portray the hazards of chemicals in the workplace as minimal, unavoidable, and acceptable. They frequently argue that workers, the public, and government regulators are overreacting so much that fear of chemicals has become a greater social problem than the hazards themselves. Belittling people who worry about chemical hazards, industry advocates call them misinformed, unscientific, emotional, and irrational. Indeed, they perceive an epidemic of "chemophobia" sweeping the nation.

Whereas labor unions describe toxic substances as deadly killers, industry downplays the risks by portraying them as unavoidable—on or off the job. Exposure to carcinogens is just a normal part of life's many hazards: Cancer-causing substances are everywhere and in everything. For example, in "Diseased Regulation," a 1979 article on OSHA's cancer policy, *Forbes* argued as follows:

> Every schoolchild can come up with a list of common, household products that cause cancer: the saccharin in a soft drink, the nitrites in a hot dog, the asbestos in insulation, the red dye in a maraschino cherry and of course the tar in a cigarette. . . . Unfortunately, it now appears that, under the "right" circumstances, any substance that can excite a cell physically can start cancerous growth. Or, as a new bumper sticker puts it: "Life Causes Cancer."
>
> That piece of folk wisdom comes a lot closer to the enormity of the problem than OSHA's [approach].[7]

Fortune attacked OSHA's cancer policy in a similar vein. Under a subheadline that read, "traces in almost everything," the magazine reported:

> [N]ot only are some vital nutrients, such as vitamin D or selenium, and long-established food preservatives, such as sodium nitrite, probable carcinogens by OSHA's standards, but the growing sensitivity of laboratory instruments enables scientists to find traces of almost anything you can name in almost anything you can eat.[8]

The examples chosen—"vital nutrients" and "long-established" food preservatives—underscore the futility of trying to eliminate exposure. Vital nutrients, of course, cannot be avoided, while long-established food preservatives have been culturally sanctioned as safe. Thus, the images suggest that attempts to prevent exposure to cancer-causing substances are foolish and doomed to failure.

Industry advocates also emphasize that chemical risks are small, using terms such as minute quantities, traces, or low doses; the implication—sometimes stated explicitly—is that if the dose is small, so is the risk. Moreover, because the risks from low-level occupational exposures are less well understood than, say, traffic hazards, industry advocates often suggest they are less real. Elizabeth Whelan, an epidemiologist and critic of federal regulatory policy, insists that it is important to distinguish between "real" and "hypothetical" risks:

> A real risk is something one can identify and quantify, then either accept or reject. Driving a car and flying in an airplane involve risks. People die. . . . Similarly, cigarettes pose a known health hazard. Epidemiological studies allow calculations of personal risk assumed here. These are real risks. The use of food additives, pesticides, and low-level exposure to occupational chemicals, on the other hand, pose hypothetical risks. Of course it is possible that they contribute to cancer mortality, but we have no evidence at this point that they do.[9]

"No evidence" can be a tactical phrase, used in controversies about technology to interpret scientific uncertainty in politically advantageous ways.[10] Concealed within the phrase are assumptions and value judgments about what constitutes evidence and proof. The phrase begs questions about the level of certainty required before we consider a "fact" to be "proven."

If, as Whelan says, "it is possible" that low-level occupational exposures cause cancer, how possible does it have to be before the evidence is valid? Are extrapolations from animal studies evidence, or is it necessary to point to human experience? Is there no evidence of a link between low-level occupational exposures and cancer, or is there no conclusive proof? Whether a risk is labeled real or hypothetical depends on answers to such value-laden questions.

If chemical risks are hypothetical, minimal, or normal, then fear of those risks is pathological and can present a serious social problem. Industry advocates denigrate public fears; *Forbes,* for example, quoted a doctor who stated

> Many people view cancer the way they viewed sex in the old Broadway melodramas: As soon as a woman had her first sexual experience, she was pregnant. One whiff of a carcinogen and you have cancer. The risk comes with repeated exposure.[11]

Business publications present government officials as anti-cancer zealots. A teaser over the *Forbes* article "Diseased Regulation" declared in boldface type that "Cancer-causing substances have acquired a satanic quality among regulators."[12] As *Fortune* explained in 1978:

> [O]f all the hazards to which the public is exposed, none seems to call forth government's natural proclivities toward overreaction so much as cancer. Politicians discern little but political risk in appearing to compromise on such an emotional issue.[13]

Comparing fears of toxic chemicals to psychological disease, industry advocates dub public concern about chemical hazards "chemophobia" or "cancerphobia." In the March 1979 issue of the U.S. Chamber of Commerce's magazine, *Nation's Business*, John W. Hanley, president of Monsanto Co., declared that the "United States is suffering from an advanced

case of chemophobia, an almost irrational fear of the products of chemistry." The article went on to explain that "much of the populace is worried about food and workplace safety, clean air and water, and, most of all, cancers thought to be by-products of chemical manufacturing."[14]

In a short opinion piece in *Chemical and Engineering News* in 1981, Don MacKinnon, president of Ciba-Geigy, echoed Hanley's concern about "chemophobia":

> What does chemophobia mean? Literally, fear of chemicals. The term generally is being used now to describe the almost spontaneous, negative response that occurs when people hear the words chemicals and chemical company. In a sense, there is almost a chemical reaction taking place when chemicals are mentioned—a flash of light accompanied by lots of smoke.[15]

In an article entitled "Chemicals and Cancerphobia" that appeared in *Society* in 1981, Elizabeth Whelan discussed the dangers of "cancerphobia":

> [T]he cancerphobia which now grips our nation and is dictating federal policy in a number of government agencies seems to be largely traceable to a fear of chemicals. A chemical anxiety. A chemical reaction.[16]

The word *phobia* implies that the fear is irrational and pathological. Politically, the use of the pejorative terms *chemophobia* and *cancerphobia* serves several tactical purposes. First, equating concern about chemicals with irrationality implies that the risks from chemical exposures are so small that rational people do not worry about them. Second, the terms undermine the credibility of those who believe that chemical risks are serious, people who (not coincidentally) are industry's political opponents. Third, these terms shift attention away from occupational disease to public fear, redefining the problem facing society.

What are the dangers of this new affliction that "grips the nation?" MacKinnon explains as follows:

> Chemophobia has had a significant impact. In the news media, with one-sided, negative stories. In the public's poor perception of the [chemical] industry. In more burdensome regulation. In higher costs and reduced productivity. In shorter patent life and lower returns on investments. In less research being done and, ultimately, in fewer drugs and other chemical entities being produced.[17]

Whelan echoes this view:

> For businessmen, the implications are clear: more regulation, higher costs, fewer jobs, and limited production. For me as a scientist and consumer the implications are also clear: high prices, higher taxes, fewer products—a diminished standard of living.[18]

In other words, the risks posed by "chemophobia" and "cancerphobia" are economic risks.[19]

Industry advocates view public relations as the solution to the problem of public fear of chemicals. In a 1983 talk entitled "If We've Done So Much, Why Are People So Worried?" Mobil executive Richard F. Tucker argued that the chemical industry should use the mass media to "educate the public" and reduce anxiety about chemicals:

> The public is still unaware of the basic points—that all life involves some risk, that there is risk in nature, that eliminating risk costs money, and that risk elimination eventually reaches a point of diminishing returns. Scientists need to explain this concept whenever they get the opportunity. . . . We must get across to the public the value of chemicals in our lives. The steady stream of scare stories has sapped public confidence in what we do and what we stand for. Scientific organizations and chemical companies alike must therefore renew their efforts to find audiences to hear their story.[20]

In reassuring advertisements and public relations material, industry presents chemicals as natural, benign, and essential to life. Monsanto ran an ad campaign that proclaimed that "Without Chemicals, Life Itself Would be Impossible."[21] A Monsanto brochure, "The Chemical Facts of Life," began in this way:

> We all depend on chemistry to live. Every breath, drop of perspiration or hunger pang involves a series of chemical reactions that are part of the life process.
>
> We live in a chemical world. Everything from the air we breathe to the earth underfoot is made of chemicals and chemical compounds.
>
> Chemicals are a fact of life.
>
> Tens of thousands of chemical compounds occur in nature and always have. Without them, there would be no world. Water is a combination of hydrogen and oxygen. Sugar is a combination of carbon, oxygen and hydrogen. Penicillin, walnuts, granite and grain—they are all chemical.[22]

The Chemical Manufacturers Association published ads that picture chemical company health and safety personnel, often with their children or grandchildren, explaining the care they take to protect our air, water, and workplaces from chemical risks.

LABOR ADVOCATES

Labor advocates describe workplace health risks in diametrically different terms—as a serious threat to the lives and well-being of many workers, their families, and their unborn children. To labor, occupational health is an enormous problem that is not being adequately addressed by society. Using powerful imagery, they stress the pain, devastation, and feeling of powerlessness that individual workers experience from occupational illnesses.

To capture the intensity of the problem, labor advocates frequently talk about an "epidemic" of occupational disease. A headline in the AFL-CIO's *Viewpoint* in 1982 referred to "A National Epidemic":

> Occupational disease is an epidemic in this country that is receiving virtually no treatment. At least 100,000 workers die each year from job-related diseases, and another 400,000 are disabled from them. But only about 5 percent of these dead or disabled receive any compensation under state workers' compensation programs.[23]

Another image used to describe the scope of the workplace health problem is that of a funeral procession. An article in the July, 1982 issue of *UFCW Action,* the newspaper of the United Food and Commercial Workers, began:

> The workplace toll is awesome and dismal. Each year the workplace bell tolls for 14,000 killed by industrial accidents and another 100,000 workers killed by job diseases.[24]

The next paragraph of the article presented another common theme: the idea that statistical aggregates are unable to describe the severity of occupational health risks.

> What the cool exactness of the statistics do [sic] not reveal is the dreadful suffering experienced by real people, by our fellow workers in so many occupations all across the country.

The article then puts human faces on the statistics by telling the stories of three "real people" who have suffered in occupational accidents or from occupational disease:

They [the statistics] don't reveal the suffering of a Barbara Angle. . . .
They don't reveal the suffering of a Leon Kruchten, a member of
UFCW Local 538. . . . They don't reveal the suffering of a Jimmy
Good, business manager for Asbestos Workers Local 11. X-rays
revealed a large mass in his lungs which doctors have diagnosed as a
cancer. The cause has been attributed to asbestos.[25]

The article continued:

None of these tragedies need have occurred. They were preventable.
Their stories and the thousands of stories like them and the untold
stories of the thousands dead indicate that much still needs to be done
to make the American workplace safe and healthy.

By stressing the number of deaths and injuries, listing the
names and stories of some "real people," and saying that these
"tragedies" were "preventable," the article paints a grim picture
of pointless human suffering on a vast scale.

Labor advocates suggest that society is ignoring its responsibility to protect workers. The article from the AFL-CIO
Viewpoint said that the "epidemic" of occupational disease is
receiving "virtually no treatment." *UFCW Action* called the
injuries "preventable," implying that they should have been
prevented. A reference to the "untold stories of the thousands
dead" suggests that society has not been listening.

For labor advocates, toxic chemicals are insidious or malev-
olent. An article in *The Chemical Worker* began "Lead, that
dull grey-colored metal is a silent killer!"[26] Focusing on the
pain and fear experienced by individuals who have been
exposed to dangerous chemicals, such metaphors stress the
idea that chemicals are foreign, that they invade the body and
contaminate people.

Images of violence or physical force express the devastating
effects of occupational disease. Toxic chemicals are called a

"time bomb," both by individual workers and in union publications. Interviewed in 1983, a worker described the chemicals he
worked with as "a time bomb ticking inside of me."[27] Former
asbestos worker James Vermeulen, head of the California-
based "Asbestos Victims of America," which has 1,900
members, told the Newark, New Jersey *Star-Ledger* that he is
suffering from the "time bomb of asbestos."[28] In May 1982,
The Chemical Worker ran an article bearing the headline
"Reproductive Hazards Called 'Time Bomb.' " The article
stated:

> Reproductive hazards have been called the 'time bomb' occupational
> health issue of the 1980's, since there may be years of delay between
> exposure to a parent and the appearance of a birth defect in his or her
> child.[29]

The time bomb image conveys the hazard as a presence that
is quietly ticking away, waiting to strike with devastating force
at some point in the future. It captures the idea of a latency
period—the time between exposure to a chemical and the
appearance of disease. It also captures the workers' uncertainty
about when the disease will appear. But the metaphor is especially disturbing because it implies that the worker is no longer
in full control of his or her body; a foreign, autonomous force
has entered it, a force that has its own predetermined course of
action, its own agenda. The worker, then, is a powerless victim
who can do nothing but listen to the ticking, wonder when the
bomb will go off, and hope that it will not be soon.

Labor advocates frequently describe occupational disease
with images of slow, painful death, of progressive deteriora-
tion, of disease that slowly spreads throughout the body. At the
1968 Congressional Hearings on the Occupational Safety and
Health Act (OSH Act) George Meany testified:

> Every year, thousands of workers die slow, often agonizing deaths
> from the effects of coal dust, asbestos, beryllium, lead, cotton dust,

carbon monoxide, cancer-causing chemicals, dyes, radiation, pesticides, and exotic fuels. Others suffer long illnesses.[30]

James Vermeulen of the Asbestos Victims of America said in 1982 that suffering from abestosis, was "like taking years to drown." That same year, the *Chicago Tribune* called attention to another metaphor used to describe abestosis:

> The disease has been likened to a spider web moving ever so slowly across the lungs. It takes up to 20 or more years to weave its debilitating web of scars, and by the time it has manifested itself in coughing and shortness of breath, little can be done to stop its frequently fatal course.[31]

The images of pain and tragedy that dominate the discourse of labor advocates sometimes give way to gallows humor. *The Chemical Worker* ran a regular column on chemical hazards called "Indecent Exposure—Are You A Victim?"[32] A cartoon in the *Labor Occupational Health Program Monitor* pictured a jug of "New! Improved, Fast Action Formula, R.I.P. Solvent" that could "Dissolve Your Troubles Away."[33]

ON ECONOMIC RISKS

INDUSTRY ADVOCATES

Industry advocates emphasize the economic risks of workplace regulation: the dangers of higher prices, fewer jobs, a lower standard of living, and stunted economic growth. They present these economic risks as a threat to the welfare of consumers, to innovation and progress, and to the survival of many businesses. Ironically, to dramatize the seriousness of these threats, they often use images of life-threatening danger.

When the OSH Act was beginning to work its way through Congress in 1968, the U.S. Chamber of Commerce's magazine, *Nation's Business*, ran an article entitled "Life or Death For Your Business," which raised the spectre of costly plant modifications, huge fines, and irresponsible federal inspectors forcing many businesses to close their gates.[34] Shortly after the Act went into effect, businesses began complaining that it threatened their continued existence. A dry cleaning firm in Idaho, for example, charged that the law:

> Imposed a financial hardship on our economy to the point where we could be closed up if we were immediately required to comply with this law completely by means of an inspection.

> There is no doubt that if the present trend in legislation continues there will be no more private ownership in business. Small business is limited to the amount of legislative controls it can withstand due to small operating capital.[35]

Business publications portray industry as being physically weakened by regulation, as if it were on the verge of collapse. *Business Week* reported in 1977 that the "steel industry, for one, is staggering under a load of 5,600 regulations from 27 different agencies—and OSHA alone accounts for 4,000 of those rules."[36] That same year, when OSHA tried to tighten standards for worker exposure to benzene, the magazine said that "companies—already reeling from the threat of benzene standards proposed by the Environmental Protection Agency— are questioning both the cost and feasibility of OSHA's move."[37]

Sometimes, in a flourish of hyperbole, industry advocates raise the spectre of complete economic collapse. Elizabeth Whelan, for example, argues:

> [W]ith today's consumer advocates leading the show, we are heading toward not only zero risk, but zero food, zero jobs, zero energy, and

zero growth. It may be that the prophets of doom, not the profits of industry, are the real hazards to our health.[38]

Images of violence, physical force, and asphyxiation dramatize the risks of regulations. In business publications, OSHA is accused of "regulatory overkill," a term that combines images of violence with the idea of excess.[39] Businesses are being "strangled" with red-tape; government regulators have a "chokehold" on industry; regulation is "stifling" progress. An advertisement by Gould Inc. that appeared in *Business Week* in 1977 illustrates this theme. The ad contained a cartoon that pictured the Statue of Liberty being hung by the neck:

> As the noose of overregulation tightens, it threatens to strangle creativity and invention—and, therefore, productivity and increased employment. To discourage risk and investment in capital expansion. To discourage increasing investment in research and development. To erode our standard of living. And, ultimately, to stifle progress.[40]

Industry advocates describe regulation as arbitrary, irrational, and unpredictable and, therefore, especially threatening. A 1978 editorial in the *Wall Street Journal*, entitled "A Low Growth Microcosm," argued that arbitrary, inconsistent, and unpredictable regulation contributes to slow economic growth: "Having to guess when this kind of regulation will strike again doesn't do much for anyone's willingness to take the risks of investment and innovation."[41] Presenting regulation as a destructive force that "strikes" virtually at random, this language emphasizes industry's concern with its lack of control.

LABOR ADVOCATES

Labor advocates have a different view of the economic risks of workplace regulation. Whereas industry emphasizes the risks to society, workers see the threats to industry profits, describing the problem in terms of "profits versus health." They charge that industry overestimates and exaggerates the cost of regulatory compliance, suggesting, on occasion, that some businesses "are not adequately informed" about OSHA regulatory procedures and are therefore prone to "irrational fears" about closing down.[42]

Labor advocates also directly counter arguments about the economic risk of workplace regulation, pointing to the risks of failing to regulate. Occupational disease is expensive, and society bears its costs through Social Security, Welfare, Medicaid, and veterans' payments.[43]

ON GOVERNMENT CONTROL OF WORKPLACE PRACTICES: REPRESSION OR PROTECTION?

INDUSTRY ADVOCATES

For industry advocates, OSHA regulation undermines industrial sovereignty; it is an illegitimate intrusion into an otherwise orderly and fair economic system. To dramatize their concerns, they present government control over workplace practices as a threat to democratic and national values and even as a form of political tyranny. OSHA thus becomes an affront to freedom and justice, an un-American institution.

For example, a 1968 article, "Life or Death for Your Business?" published in *Nation's Business*, warned that, if enacted, the OSH Act would arm "federal 'inspectors'" with "the power of life or death over your business."[44] The article began with the following fantasy:

> Imagine yourself sitting in your office a few months from today. A young man barges in. You recognize him as a man you once refused to

hire. He had no education and no potential talent you could use. His main experience consisted of cashing welfare checks.

But he shows you he's now a representative of the federal government—an "inspector" with the Department of Labor.

And he threatens to padlock your gates and have you fined $1,000 a day if you don't do as he says.

The young man—who knows nothing about your business—then tramps through your plant, without a warrant, ordering you to take costly steps to improve "safety and health."

Such scenes could be duplicated throughout the country if a new proposal being deliberated on Capitol Hill be signed into law.[45]

This passage skillfully presents OSHA as a threat to democratic values. The inspector is a man with broad and formidable powers, unbounded by the requirements of due process of law. Aggressive verbs describe his action: He "barges in" and "tramps through . . . without a warrant." Moreover, the passage strongly implies that OSHA inspectors might use their power to conduct unjust personal vendettas against business. Thus, OSHA becomes an extreme example of illegitimate authority.

Industry advocates also present government health and safety regulation as un-American. A business manager from Lawrence, Kansas, for example, complained in 1972:

[A]n inspector from the Dept. of Labor can come into my plant at any time, make an inspection and then demand changes without regard to cost or need. At the same time this inspector can levy fines of up to $1,000.00 a day or this same agency, the Dept. of Labor, can shut down a portion of or the entire operation. There is also, as always, the threat of imprisonment. Our representatives in Washington have given this Agency the authority to accuse, try, judge, and sentence us on the spot! I would wonder if this is constitutional? Are we still in America?[46]

During the early years of OSHA, industry advocates argued that OSHA regulation had created a "police state," charging at one point that OSHA regulation was being administered "in a high-handed, dictatorial manner . . . reminiscent of the days of Mr. Hitler in Germany."[47] In 1972, Senator Clifford P. Hansen charged that in Wyoming, his home state, people were

> actually . . . losing their jobs. I have letters in my office—I can show them—not from employers, but from employees, who say if this law is enforced "I am going to be out of work because my employer is not going to run the risk of Gestapo tactics"—and I underscore that word, because that is exactly what it is. . . . It is a police state. These people come in. They are the inspectors. They are the judge and jury. They levy fines. . . . They have scared the living daylights out of more businessmen than will ever be known.[48]

In recent years industry advocates have refrained from such extreme comparisons, but they continue to describe workplace regulation as an illegitimate use of government power. They frequently complain about OSHA's "regulatory fiat." *Business Week*, for example, described the issue of who should control workplace health and safety practices as a "battle over industry discretion vs. OSHA's fiat,"[49] thereby contrasting judicious and considered management policy with authoritarian and arbitrary government control.

LABOR ADVOCATES

Labor advocates argue that limited control over industry's practices leaves employees powerless and vulnerable; workplace regulation is necessary to protect workers from predatory industrial managers. Reflecting a strong historical mistrust of industry, labor advocates believe that business will ruthlessly exploit workers in any manner that the law allows.

Thus, they perceive health and safety regulation, along with union contract negotiations,[50] as protection against injustice.

Describing OSHA as a result of the long campaign against unsafe working conditions, labor advocates argue, as one bumper sticker states, "OSHA SAVES LIVES." The UAW's paper, *Solidarity*, reported in 1981: "Since 1970, when the Occupational Safety & Health Act . . . became law, the number of job-related illnesses, accidents, and deaths has dropped."[51] The Connecticut Union of Telephone Workers echoed this view in the *CUTW Union Voice:*

> Although labor may feel OSHA isn't perfect and sometimes compromising [sic], it has made innumerable jobs safer. Between 1972 and 1979, job-related injuries, illnesses, and deaths were cut by 15 percent by its efforts and inspections.[52]

Crediting OSHA with reducing the lead levels in the blood of workers in a battery manufacturing plant, UAW activist Glen Odom said, "None of this would have happened without OSHA's new lead standard. We were facing the possibility of deformed kids—this stuff's pure poison. So OSHA's been just great for us."[53]

Labor advocates are thus deeply concerned about the Reagan administration's cutbacks in the agency. They argue that the administration and its congressional supporters are "gutting the OSHA enforcement program" as part of "the conservative political agenda to subsidize the business community at the expense of workers."[54] They emphasize that they have nowhere else to turn. As an article in *Solidarity* put it: "Asking OSHA to protect workers these days is a little like asking Scrooge for a Christmas present—but necessity bends us to the task."[55]

Using images of violence and asphyxiation, labor advocates accuse the Reagan administration of "strangling" or "slowly choking OSHA to death."[56] The *CUTW Union Voice* reported in 1982 that OSHA "is reeling but hanging on gamely as pugilist President Ronald Reagan and his seconds pound it into the ropes."[57] An article in the *UFCW Action* charged that "safety and health are being bulldozed out of the American workplace." Underneath, a graphic pictured a bulldozer operator wearing an executioner's mask driving his machine into a group of screaming people who were labeled "OSHA," while typewriters, telephones, and laboratory equipment flew through the air.[58] To labor advocates, workers are the victims—for without strong OSHA regulation, workers will have no protection. As UAW President Douglas A. Fraser put it, under Reagan's OSHA, "law and order stops at the plant gates."[59]

ON THE IMPERATIVES THAT MUST GUIDE ACTION: ECONOMIC OR MORAL?

INDUSTRY ADVOCATES

Central to the occupational health controversy is the choice of considerations that must guide social policy. Industry advocates emphasize the economic nature of decisions about worker protection. Regarding safety and health as economic commodities, they stress the need to make cost-benefit choices. Using the language and paradigms of economics, they frame the issue as a problem of efficiency: How can society best invest its limited resources? How can money spent on safety be spent most effectively? How much health and safety can we afford?

The argument goes as follows: It is impossible to achieve "zero risk," for "safe" is a relative term. Because perfect safety is impossible, we must balance demands for increased safety against the cost of meeting them. Government regulators and the public are seeking the unattainable, and therefore irrational, goal of perfect safety. As *Forbes* put it: "No matter what single-minded regulators . . . may think, risk can't be eliminated from life."[60]

Because risk cannot be eliminated, industry advocates argue that it should be reduced to "acceptable" levels. Risk reduction inevitably reaches a point of diminishing returns, where additional expenditures will not lower risk substantially. Therefore, society must decide whether the risk is "acceptable" or whether more should be spent to reduce it further. To make such choices, society should carefully analyze the costs and benefits of risk control. Otherwise, risk reduction will damage the economy.

Industry advocates contend that many OSHA regulations are inefficient, with costs that greatly outweigh benefits. For example, *Nation's Business* reported in 1980 that "the chemical industry has calculated that OSHA's proposed limits on worker exposure to benzene would eliminate one case of leukemia every six years, at a cost of $300 million."[61] Such misallocations of resources, industry argues, can actually reduce the overall safety of society.

> A society never has enough resources to do everything that everyone would like to do. But OSHA and its brethren are not responsible for weighing their own plans against alternative uses of resources outside their spheres of influence. Thus, OSHA's efforts to save lives . . . may result in a net loss of lives.[62]

There is a linkage between economic risks and health risks, say industry advocates; inefficient regulation increases both.

Framing the occupational health issue in economic terms is politically advantageous for industry. First, by defining the problem as one of scarce resources, industry advocates emphasize the inevitable constraints on social action. This allows them to embrace the general goals of health and safety while opposing specific worker protection measures that they believe are not cost-effective. It shifts the blame for occupational disease from the deliberate choices of industrial managers to economic imperatives. As limits are imposed by the situation—not by immoral, profit-hungry bosses—they provide a natural law defense; industry cannot be held culpable.

Second, the emphasis on maximizing the *number* of lives saved draws attention away from the question of *whose* lives will be saved, downplaying the moral issues raised by the unequal distribution of risk. Expensive worker protection measures are not seen as a means of redressing this imbalance, but as inefficient allocation of resources. Labor is presented as a special interest that is demanding more than its share.

LABOR ADVOCATES

In their discourse labor advocates emphasize the moral content of decisions about worker protection. Employing the language of rights, they justify their views in the name of fairness and decency; life and health are inalienable rights that society has a responsibility to defend. Recognizing that it is impossible to eliminate risk completely, they argue that society must protect workers from health hazards whenever feasible. Thus, they challenge cost-benefit analyses that attempt to balance the cost of worker protection against the number of lives saved. Instead, they stress equity, saying that society has a moral obligation to protect workers from the risks they are forced to bear.

Testifying before Congress in support of the OSH Act in 1968, Clinton M. Fair of the AFL-CIO argued that workers have a "right to a safe workplace":

> We hold it self-evident that every man and woman should be furnished, insofar as is humanly possible, a safe place to work. Yet it is an unchallenged fact that this basic right is flagrantly violated.[63]

Beyond the right to health, labor advocates also argue that workers have a right to know about job hazards. As John Odorcich of the United Steelworkers of America (USWA) told Congress in 1981:

> The right-to-know is not a difficult concept. It simply means that American workers should have access to accurate information about the identity and the hazards of the materials they use. As we have tried to show, the right-to-know is a matter of public health. But it is also a matter of human rights and human dignity in the workplace.[64]

Using strong language, labor advocates denounce violations of these rights. Nate Ferry of the USWA, for example, made this statement:

> The company does not buy [a worker's] body for an hourly rate, a paycheck for a life. Nowhere is that a condition of work. When you send people out in these various areas of plants to work with toxic substances that have low flash points, toxicity and hydrocarbons which are carcinogens, and expose these people to this without any knowledge whatsoever—you would treat an animal better than that.[65]

Framing the occupational health issue in terms of rights is politically advantageous for labor advocates. Rights have two important characteristics. First, people are endowed with rights simply because they are human and, therefore, in theory rights are equally distributed. A laborer in an oil refinery has the same right to health as an executive in an air-conditioned suite. Second, the concept of rights conveys a moral imperative: A person's rights cannot legitimately be denied except through extraordinary procedures, such as due process in a court of law. Arguing that workers' rights are "flagrantly violated," labor advocates call into question the morality of industry officials and the legitimacy of current systems of workplace control.

By defining occupational health as an issue of justice rather than economic efficiency, labor advocates challenge the idea that society must balance the cost of workplace regulation against the value of the lives saved. They also question the ability to place a dollar value on human life. Labor Secretary W. Willard Wirtz expressed this theme at the 1968 Congressional hearings on the OSH Act:

> It is going to be a very fair question of those who oppose S. 2864 on the basis of cost and expense to ask them just exactly what they regard as the price of human life or a limb, or an eye, and whether they would consider the price the same for a member of any family in America as they would for their own family.[66]

In this view cost-benefit analysis becomes "a moral outrage when applied to human life."[67] Speaking at a 1981 Congressional hearing, Nolan W. Hancock of the Oil, Chemical, and Atomic Workers said that his union "has protested and will continue to protest the immorality of putting workers' lives and health into an economic cost-benefit equation."[68]

In this moral context, the notion of "acceptable risk" is in itself unjust. Sheldon W. Samuels of the AFL-CIO argued in 1978 that establishing "acceptable risk" amounts to the

> creation of a class of expendables, seldom humanely selected or compensated. These are cannibalized groups selected for sacrifice by someone or some group with the belief or the assumption or the rationalization that for the sake of the greatest number, the few can be "acceptably" sacrificed. Seldom are the expendables consulted.[69]

Samuels argued that although some risks may be "necessary," they should not be termed "acceptable."[70]

THEORIES OF SOCIETY:
CONSENSUS OR CONFLICT?

INDUSTRY ADVOCATES

Underlying the discourse of industry advocates is a "theory" of society that emphasizes consensus, common goals, and confluence—rather than conflict—of interests. They stress that protecting workers' health is an interest shared by management and labor. Viewing the economic system as reasonable, efficient, and nonexploitative, they describe conflict and adversary relationships as disruptive of the social process through which decisions routinely are made.

Industry advocates build their case for a confluence of interests by stressing their concern about worker health and safety, documenting industry efforts to improve the protection of employees. During the 1968 hearings on the OSH Act John O. Logan of the Manufacturing Chemists' Association (later renamed the Chemical Manufacturers Association) testified:

> [C]ontinuing strides in occupational safety and health have been achieved through the voluntary efforts of businessmen, both individually and through trade associations, during decades of record industrial growth. . . . The Manufacturing Chemists' Association not only subscribes to the objectives of enhancing the safety and well-being of workers—indeed, it has been a pioneer in this field.[71]

Testifying before Congress in 1981 on behalf of the Chemical Manufacturers Association (CMA), Curtis W. Smith echoed the same theme: "As a result of continuing concern by CMA and member companies, the chemical industry has one of the most outstanding safety records in American industry."[72] Cases of industry carelessness or malfeasance are seen as unusual and atypical. The following comment from Mobil executive Richard F. Tucker illustrates this theme:

> With very rare exceptions, industry *did* abide by [government controls on the chemical industry] conscientiously. As a result, the products which the chemical industry makes, and the plants where it makes them, are better and safer than before. We can properly take credit for a job well done.[73]

The director of health and safety for Du Pont expressed a similar view:

> The chemical industry has much to be proud of in its commitment to and performance in safety and health. . . . But both you and I know that in any field the excellent results of the 99% who are responsible are quickly forgotten when the remaining 1% make mistakes, are thoughtless or are just plain irresponsible. I could praise the industry and you could quickly point to the exceptions.[74]

This line of argument dismisses illegal, unethical, or careless practices as the ill-advised acts of a few irresponsible individuals or firms rather than viewing them as evidence of a structural problem in the industry.

The consensus view of the social process is reflected in the repeated use of the pronouns "we" and "our." Instead of asking what is in management's or labor's best interest, industry advocates ask what is in "our" best interest, as if everyone were on the same side. Elizabeth Whelan provides an example:

> All of *us* are in favor of good health. If a chemical or processing technique, or any other aspect of *our* environment, threatens *our* health, *we* would all be in favor of restricting or curtailing its use.[75] (emphasis added)

Similarly, industry advocates stress the common interest in reducing economic risks: They are borne by "society at large."

Curtis W. Smith of the CMA told Congress that "as the American public has painfully learned, unnecessarily complex regulation generates costs that are borne by society at large (which includes workers) and not solely by stockholders of regulated corporations."[76] Whelan writes: "*We* are heading toward . . . zero growth."[77] Gould Inc. warns in an advocacy advertisement that "overregulation" threatens to "erode *our* standard of living."[78] (emphases added) The notion of a confluence of interests is reinforced by arguments that regulations ultimately will affect employment by increasing the threat of foreign competition—a sensitive issue for workers and one of the points of agreement between labor and management.

Industry advocates assume that everyone benefits from the existing economic system. Business provides workers jobs and income; economic growth and progress raise everyone's standard of living; and when business is doing well, the benefits "trickle down" to the rest of the community. Rejecting the idea that different groups within society might have fundamentally different interests, industry advocates challenge the implication that the economic system can be exploitative or that the profit motive can lead to neglect of workers' health and safety.

These arguments often are defensive. In 1968, a critic of the OSH Act complained that the proposed law had "a sort of 'why don't you stop beating your wife' orientation."[79] A businessman objected in 1972 that the OSH Act "assumes that I am in business to try to make money by working people in unsafe places and jobs, using unsafe tools. It practically accuses me of hiring employees for the purpose of maiming and killing them."[80]

Instead of producing a conflict of interests, industry sees the profit motive as a source of consensus. As *Nation's Business* put it:

> The private sector is motivated by profits to seek safer working conditions and products. That profit incentive will reduce the accident and disease rate to the lowest level consistent with an efficient allocation of resources. . . . Unsafe working conditions can deprive an employer of

trained workers, increase insurance costs, and raise wages for dangerous work.[81]

Similarly, to industry advocates technological development
is by definition in the common interest, bringing a wide variety
of new and better products, from better crops to life-saving
drugs, from versatile plastics to convenient transportation. In
its booklet, "The Chemical Facts of Life," Monsanto presented
the following vision of progress and technological development:

> Cavemen huddled around a fire may seem an unlikely place to begin a
> discussion of the benefits of chemistry. But the first time a spark was
> struck to light a fire, people were using chemistry to their benefit. Fire
> is the result of a chemical reaction.
>
> Ever since that first spark, advances in chemistry have been contribut-
> ing to human progress. . . . [The] resulting products have contributed
> to improving people's lives.[82]

As a corollary to the emphasis on common interests in
occupational health, cooperative decision making becomes a
goal; for adversarial procedures will only interfere with
rational decision making. Monsanto expressed this viewpoint
in "The Chemical Facts of Life" in a section called "Who
Decides?" The company argued that in order to make good
decisions about toxic chemicals:

> we must have more cooperation and less confrontation. With increas-
> ing frequency groups with different opinions find themselves in bruis-
> ing adversarial conflicts. These conflicts are conducive to highlighting
> differences, but they are largely ineffective in finding reasonable solu-
> tions based on fact. . . .
>
> Ways must be found so that producers, regulators and users of chemi-
> cals can, cooperatively, reach the best decisions possible.
>
> At times, the process may break down. Adversarial relationships may
> be necessary in legal and administrative proceedings, but it is unpro-
> ductive to begin decision-making at the most contentious point.

Cooperation may take a change in attitude on everyone's part, but it is the only reasonable way to reach important decisions.[83]

Adversarial relationships are unproductive; occurring when the consensus process breaks down, they do not contribute to "reasonable solutions."

How do industry advocates reconcile their theory of consensus with the existence of conflict over workplace health and safety? Rather than rejecting their theory, they argue that conflict stems from people's "irrational fears" about chemicals. As Monsanto put it:

Emotion and fear can further complicate decision-making. In the case of chemicals, legitimate concerns about a few chemicals have become, for some people, general fears about all chemicals. In the highly charged atmosphere that results, there can be demands for immediate action—an attempt to resolve scientific questions by legislative or regulatory fiat.[84]

Emotion and fear, in other words, blur the vision of some individuals, making it difficult for them to perceive the confluence of interests that really exists. Adversarial relationships in occupational health, therefore, are caused by uninformed, unscientific, or irrational individuals, not by fundamentally different interests.

Just as industry advocates blame pathological individuals for conflict, so too do they blame OSHA, a pathological government agency. They present OSHA as irrational, unreasonable, burdensome, politically unpopular, and a threat to orderly, consensus-based decision making. They attack the agency aggressively, with sarcasm and strong language. The following example, from a *Fortune* article entitled "Must OSHA Make Sense?" is typical:

Poor OSHA! The folks who run the Occupational Safety and Health Administration have been long reconciled to the fact that nobody out there loves them. What's bothering them now is something far more serious. They confront the chilling prospect that [due to court actions], sometime in the next few months, the agency's rulings will have to begin making sense. The costs it imposes on business may actually have to bear some relation to the benefits.[85]

Fortune titled another article "OSHA's Ill-Conceived Crusade Against Cancer."[86] *Business Week* described the agency as "a blindly regulating body that ignores costs and common sense."[87]

Industry advocates frequently use humor to ridicule the agency, for example, by listing regulations that appear silly. An article in *Nation's Business* called violations of OSHA regulations "safety booboo[s]," giving the following list:

Suppose the rungs of your ladder are made from the wrong kind of wood or are not spaced far enough apart.

The ladder won't pass the Occupational Safety and Health Administration's meticulous standards.

Could be that your sheepherders aren't close enough to the men's room.

Maybe there's no guardrail around your picture window.[88]

Finally, industry advocates define the agency as controversial. *Nation's Business* reported that OSHA was "perhaps the least loved of federal agencies."[89] *Business Week* called OSHA "the federal regulator most bitterly criticized by business," charging—some eight years after OSHA's inception—that the "beleaguered" agency was "still trying to get its act together."[90] The long list of unflattering adjectives used to characterize OSHA's regulations includes the following: nonsensical, nitpicking, niggling, unnecessary, unmanageable, unrealistic, unreasonable, irrational, irritating, irrelevant, ridiculous, cumbersome, exasperating, and extreme.[91]

LABOR ADVOCATES

In contrast to a theory of society that stresses consensus and a confluence of interests, labor advocates emphasize conflict between interest groups. They see workplace politics as governed by adversarial relationships, and they question the extent of management's stake in protecting workers' health. They describe the economic system as exploitative, charging that companies trade workers' lives for profits. They accuse industry of withholding information about health risks to keep the workforce docile. Society is coercive and decision making is biased against the working class.

Convinced that workers and industry have different interests in occupational health, labor advocates argue that industry's primary concern, containing costs, limits efforts to protect employees. At the 1968 Congressional hearings on the OSH Act Ralph Nader argued that federal regulation of workplace health and safety was necessary:

There is strong evidence to suggest that there is a certain threshold level of concern held by many of these companies, that they will work up to a certain level, in terms of reducing some of the deaths and injuries, but then there comes a certain cutoff point beyond which the incentives or disincentives simply don't operate to make them engage in the required investment, and the required work practices, to push this death and injury level down lower.[92]

According to Nader, this problem of a threshold level of concern was most serious for chronic occupational disease.

If an injury is visible, if you can smell it, see it, if you can be repelled by it visually, industry tends to be more careful in this area, but . . . much of the occupational health problem today is invisible. It is the kind of hazard that leads to cancer, to respiratory diseases, cell destruction, heart ailments, bladder cancers, and so forth . . . it is of the long-range, invisible, relatively insidious impact-type.[93]

Focusing on conflicting interests, labor advocates charge that industry is not sufficiently concerned with job-related disease because it does not bear its full cost. According to an article in the AFL-CIO *Viewpoint:*

> It's not the industries responsible for occupational disease that usually pay [to care for and compensate victims]. . . . Until employers are required to shoulder the full burden for occupational diseases, they will have no economic incentive to improve job safety and health.[94]

Workplace health programs, say labor advocates, reflect the priorities of management, not workers. In 1982 *The Chemical Worker* gave this account of industry's motives:

> Companies perform medical tests to protect themselves, not to protect you. The company doc cares about the financial health of the company, not your physical health. Workers are given exams for very specific reasons: (1) to insure productivity by screening out workers unable to perform the jobs they will be assigned to; (2) to try to block later compensation claims or to minimize the size of the award; (3) because they're forced to by certain OSHA standards, like the lead standard; (4) to harass and discriminate against workers the company wants to get rid of.[95]

Labor advocates often accuse industry of exploiting workers, trading workers' health and lives for profits. They portray business as corrupt and venal. A cartoon in the *Labor Occupational Health Program Monitor* pictured an industrialist emptying a wastebasket full of workers into a trash can.[96] Sydney Wolfe of the Health Research Group called occupational injury and disease "the leading form of violence, domestic or foreign."[97] An article in the United Auto Workers' *Solidarity* said that business interests had "put OSHA at the top of their hit list because they didn't like spending even the relatively small bit of their profits that OSHA compliance required."[98]

Mistrusting the paternalistic policies of industry and concerned that workers lack information about health hazards, labor advocates attack business for misleading workers and violating their right to know. "Industry cannot be relied upon to provide voluntarily the information that workers need to protect their health and that of their children."[99] They support this assertion by pointing to cases in which industry failed to inform workers about hazards when they first were discovered.[100] Individual workers bitterly complain that their trust was violated. James Vermeulen of the Asbestos Victims of America charged that his employers knew about the health hazards of asbestos: "They've known. They never told me in 1957 that, Jim, this stuff might make [you] sick. . . . I trusted industry, but they knew. They knew all along."[101]

Labor advocates contend that industry resists giving workers complete information on hazardous chemicals in order to keep them under control. In a 1977 article the United Auto Workers' *Occupational Health and Safety Newsletter* charged:

> Obtaining information about chemicals that workers face on the job remains one of the biggest problems of health and safety. Too often the very names of chemicals are withheld from workers. The smokescreen of "trade secrets" is often used to hide facts about potentially dangerous chemicals in the plant.[102]

A representative of the United Steelworkers of America told Congress in 1981:

> Workers who want to know what they are working with are told: "It won't hurt you," or "It's safe when used as directed," or "We can't get that information from our supplier," or "You wouldn't understand anyway," or "Management is not required to reveal that information." Of these five statements, only the last is generally accurate.[103]

Calling the lack of information "deliberately imposed industrial ignorance,"[104] labor advocates charge that withholding information is a form of coercion:

If the workers do not know the nature of the dangers assaulting them in the workplace, they will not be in a position to challenge their employers, file a complaint with OSHA, or take other legal action towards compensation. This is the crux of the "right to know" controversy. An informed worker takes action. A worker who is kept in the dark is complacent.[105]

Concern about coercion is central to the discourse of labor advocates. They charge that many of those who face high risks on the job have limited employment options, are poorly paid, and are inadequately compensated for injuries. Moreover, minorities hold a disproportionate number of dangerous jobs. A 1981 article in *The Chicago Reporter*, a paper specializing in racial issues, charged:

There is an industrial time bomb exploding and minority workers may be at the center of the blast. . . . Emerging evidence suggests that one solution to the mystery of sharply rising cancer rates among minorities may be found in the workplace.[106]

Labor advocates argue that the threat of being fired and the fear of unemployment coerce workers into accepting health risks, especially in small, nonunion shops. Reporting on interviews with workers, *The Chicago Reporter*, for example, suggested that many employees "feel powerless to change unhealthy conditions because, in the current economic climate, they know they are easily replaced. Fear of being fired prevents them from speaking publicly about their jobs."[107]

Perceiving possible conflicts of interest, labor advocates are ambivalent about the introduction of new chemicals into the workplace. While industry describes the development of new chemicals as innovation and progress,[108] labor points out that

technological change has brought new, greater prominence to a different class of hazards—chemical hazards. Toxic chemicals pose new problems for workers in evaluating the risks they face in their jobs.[109]

They are concerned that new risks may not be recognized and controlled. A representative of the Oil, Chemical, and Atomic Workers told Congress in 1981:

> Thousands of new chemicals are coming in the workplace each year. We cannot allow today's analogs of benzidine and beta naphthylamine and asbestos to produce an epidemic among uninformed workers and their offspring 10 to 20 years from now.[110]

At the same hearings, a representative of the International Association of Fire Fighters warned that the problem of protecting workers from new chemicals "may worsen since modern technology has proved capable of producing new substances faster than science can determine their toxic effects."[111]

Throughout their discourse, labor advocates stress conflicts of interest, unfairness and inequity, and coercion. In keeping with this emphasis, they describe the social process through which decisions are made as a contest between competing groups. They talk of the "fight" for stronger health regulations. They write of "The Battle For Workplace Safety."[112] They present themselves as the underdogs in a struggle against injustice that pits workers against powerful industrialists.

CONCLUSION

Examining the divergent perceptions of industry and labor advocates reveals a set of contradictory beliefs—about the social relationships, government control, severity of risks, and the imperatives that should guide policy. These conflicting beliefs, based on opposing political myths, obstruct the resolution of the problem of occupational health. Opposing views of health and economic risks, amplified by scientific uncertainty, limit the possibilities for negotiation. Similarly, disagreements about the extent of common interests and the proper role of government regulation preclude the development of a common framework for resolving disputes. Finally, the debate about which imperatives should guide social policy tends to ignore the tensions between the allocation of resources and the rights of individuals. Claims that social choices should be viewed as *either* economic decisions *or* as moral ones obscure rather than illuminate the issues.[113]

The contradictory views of industry and labor advocates constitute two opposing clusters of political myths. The myths in each cluster are interrelated and form a coherent ideological framework. Moreover, each myth can evoke an entire set of related questions. The statement that workers face "terrible risks" refers to the belief that health risks are serious, but it also raises questions about why they face these risks, who is to blame, and what should be done. Answers are provided by the other myths in the cluster—about the exploitation of workers, the immorality of industrial managers, and the need for government protection. Similarly, the charge that people have "irrational fears" about chemicals evokes not only the belief that health risks are minimal, but also myths about the benevolence of industry, the dangers of government control, and the threat posed by deviant individuals.

The political discourse thus reveals two internally consistent but irreconcilable clusters of myths. These opposing ideologies, and the deep conflict between labor and industry that they reflect, obstruct resolution. As the prospects for negotiation are limited, policy outcomes will depend primarily on the ability of each group to impose its will.

In this struggle for power ideology becomes strategically important and, in addition to forming a barrier to resolution, the opposing clusters of myths become political resources. Using language, operatives can evoke familiar myths, constructing emotional public dramas to win political support. Thus, despite their sharp ideological differences, industry and labor use similar tactics in public debate.

- Each group uses graphic, emotional imagery, filled with references to violence and death, to dramatize its version of risks.

- Each uses images that emphasize its lack of control over the risks and situations that threaten it.

- Each accuses the other of exaggerating, calling the other side's case histories "scare stories" or "horror stories."[114]

- Each presents itself in a favorable light, while calling its political opponents irrational or immoral and identifying them as a source of social problems.

- Each evokes widely shared values—such as prosperity, health, freedom, justice, efficiency, and equity—to position itself on the "right" side of the controversy.

- Each group argues that its viewpoint is based on careful analysis of "facts." As a corollary to this assertion, both groups treat science and expertise as political resources, invoking the conclusions and opinions of specialists as tools for persuasion.

In this manner, each group constructs a dramatic picture of the occupational health controversy, presenting an image of society and social institutions, naming heroes and villains, identifying certain "problems" as urgent and others as less urgent, and proposing "solutions" to the problems it defines.

At its deepest level the debate over occupational health reflects a dispute about the legitimacy of existing economic and political arrangements and of current systems of workplace control. Thus, the strongly held views of each group cannot be easily dispelled either by political rhetoric or by technical information. Occupational health, therefore, is likely to remain a contentious issue, the subject of a persistent, acerbic, and highly stylized debate.

NOTES

1. The term ideology has been used in many different ways. Here it is used to refer to symbolic structures: intricate webs of interacting symbols that provide streamlined, schematic maps of problematic social reality. For a discussion, see Clifford Geertz, "Ideology as a Cultural System," in *The Interpretation of Cultures*, ed. C. Geertz (New York: Basic Books, 1973).

2. Murray Edelman, *Political Language* (New York: Academic Press, 1977), pp. 6-7.

3. George Lakoff and Mark Johnson, *Metaphors We Live By* (Chicago: University of Chicago Press, 1980), p. 5.

4. See, for example, Lakoff and Johnson's discussion of the metaphor INFLATION IS AN ADVERSARY. Ibid., pp. 33-34.

5. Barry Crickmer, "Regulation: How Much Is Enough?" *Nation's Business,* March 1980, p. 27.

6. See, for example, Ruth Ruttenberg and Randall Hudgins, *Occupational Safety and Health in the Chemical Industry* (New York: Council on Economic Priorities, 1981).

7. "Diseased Regulation," *Forbes,* February 1979, p. 34.

8. Tom Alexander, "OSHA's Ill-Conceived Crusade Against Cancer," *Fortune,* 3 July 1978, p. 87.

9. Elizabeth M. Whelan, "Chemicals and Cancerphobia," *Society,* March/April 1981, p. 7.

10. For a discussion of the use of the term "no evidence" in the nuclear controversy, see Stephen Hilgartner, Richard C. Bell, and Rory O'Connor, *Nukespeak* (San Francisco: Sierra Club Books, 1982).

11. "Diseased Regulation," p. 34.

12. Ibid.

13. Alexander, "OSHA's Ill-Conceived Crusade," p. 87.

14. Michael Thoryn, "Chemicals & Plastics: The Catalysts of Living," *Nation's Business,* March 1979, p. 70.

15. Don MacKinnon, "Chemophobia," *Chemical and Engineering News,* 13 July 1981, p. 5.

16. Whelan, "Chemicals and Cancerphobia," p. 8.

17. Mackinnon, "Chemophobia," p. 5.

18. Whelan, "Chemicals and Cancerphobia," p. 8.

19. As noted below, industry advocates perceive a linkage between health and economic risks.

20. Richard F. Tucker, "If We've Done So Much, Why are People So Worried?" (Paper delivered at the Annual Meeting of the Chemical Industry Institute of Toxicology, March 16, 1983), pp. 7-8.

21. For a discussion of Monsanto's campaign by two advertising specialists, see Al Ries and Jack Trout, *Positioning* (New York: McGraw Hill, 1981).

22. Monsanto Company, "The Chemical Facts of Life," brochure, p. 1.

23. "Needed: Workers Compensation for Occupational Disease," AFL-CIO *Viewpoint,* Spring 1982, p. 19

24. "We Just Come to Work Here: We Don't Come to Die," *UFCW Action,* July/August 1982, p. 16.

25. Barbara Angle and Leon Kruchten were injured in industrial accidents. Angle's arm was crushed under a coal shuttle. Kruchten lost his arm due to burns received from a severe electric shock.

26. "Get the Lead Out! It Can Kill You!" *The Chemical Worker,* January 1982, p. 7.

27. Dorothy Nelkin and Michael S. Brown, *Workers at Risk* (Chicago: University of Chicago Press, 1984), p. 181.

28. Robert G. Seidenstein, "State Justices Face Landmark Case on Asbestos Exposure," (Newark, NJ) *Star-Ledger,* 4 April 1982.

29. "Reproductive Hazards Called 'Time Bomb,' " *The Chemical Worker,* May 1982, p. 11.

30. Quoted in Steven Kelman, "Occupational Safety and Health Administration," in *The Politics of Regulation,* ed. James Q. Wilson (New York: Basic Books, 1980), p. 243.

31. Robert Kearns, "Asbestos Days Still Haunt UNR," *Chicago Tribune,* 31 March 1982.

32. *The Chemical Worker,* 1982.

33. *Labor Occupational Health Program Monitor* (July 1982), p. 1.

34. "Life or Death For Your Business?" *Nation's Business,* April 1968.

35. U.S. Congress, Senate, Committee on Labor and Public Welfare, *Implementation of the Occupational Health and Safety Act, 1972* (Hearings before the Subcommittee on Labor, 92nd Congress, 2nd session, July 25, 26, 27, September 19, 1972) p. 433 (hereafter cited as *Senate Hearings,* 1972).

36. "OSHA: Hardest To Live With," *Business Week,* 4 April 1977, p. 79.

37. "What Benzene's Link to Leukemia Will Cost," *Business Week,* 9 May 1977, p. 35.

38. Whelan, "Chemicals and Cancerphobia," p. 8.

39. "OSHA: Hardest To Live With," p. 79.

40. Gould Inc., advertisement in *Business Week,* 27 November 1978.

41. "A Low Growth Microcosm," *Wall Street Journal,* 10 October 1978, p. 22.

42. Sydney Wolfe, statement before the Subcommittee on Labor, *Senate Hearings,* 1972, pp. 294-295.

43. "Needed: Workers' Compensation," AFL-CIO *Viewpoint,* p. 19.

44. "Life Or Death For Your Business?" *Nation's Business.*

45. Ibid.

46. Lee Scott to J. D. Hodgson, Department of Labor, February 7, 1972, in *Senate Hearings,* 1972, p. 127.

47. *Senate Hearings,* 1972, p. 336.

48. Ibid., p. 82.

49. "OSHA: Hardest To Live With," p. 79.

50. Government plays an important role here, too, through federal labor laws.

51. "Don't Let This Bumper Sticker Become Obsolete!" UAW *Solidarity,* 1-15 December 1981, p. 24.

52. Liz Barzda, "Down But Not Out—OSHA Fighting Back," *CTWU Union Voice,* June 1982, p. 4.

53. Jeff Stansbury, "The Battle For Workplace Safety," UAW *Solidarity,* 1-15 December 1981, p. 12.

54. "We Just Come To Work Here." p. 18.

55. "UAW, Other Unions Ask Job Protection From Formaldehyde," UAW *Solidarity,* 1-15 December 1981, p. 14.

56. See, for example, UAW *Solidarity,* 1-15 December 1981, pp. 12, 24.

57. Barzda, "Down But Not Out," p. 4.

58. "We Just Come To Work Here." pp. 16-17.

59. Stansbury, "The Battle For Workplace Safety," p. 12.

60. "Diseased Regulation."

61. Crickmer, "Regulation: How Much Is Enough?," p. 32.

62. Ibid.

63. U.S. Congress, Senate, Committee on Labor and Public Welfare, *Occupational Safety and Health Act of 1968* (Hearings before the Subcommittee on Labor, 90th Congress, 2nd session, February 15, June 6, 12, 19, 24, 28, and July 2, 1968), p. 483 (hereafter cited as *Senate Hearings*, 1968).

64. U.S. Congress, House, Committee on Education and Labor, *OSHA Oversight Hearings on Proposed Rules on Hazards Identification* (Hearings before the Subcommittee on Health and Safety, 97th Congress, 1st session, April 7, 28, May 19, 27, July 8, 14, 21, and October 6, 1981), p. 250 (hereafter cited as *House Hearings, 1981*).

65. Ibid., p. 3.

66. *Senate Hearings*, 1968, p. 62.

67. Vernon M. Jensen, *House Hearings*, 1981, p. 134.

68. *House Hearings*, 1981, p. 103.

69. Sheldon W. Samuels, "The Fallacies of Acceptable Risk," in *Risk/Benefit Decisions and the Public Health*, Proceedings of the Third FDA Science Symposium, February 15-17, 1978, HEW Publication (FDA) 80-1069, p. 174.

70. Ibid., pp. 174-177.

71. *Senate Hearings*, 1968, p. 255.

72. *House Hearings*, 1981, p. 250.

73. Tucker, "If We've Done So Much," p. 1.

74. Parry M. Norling, "Health and Safety in the Chemical Industry," (Paper given at the Chemical Industry Seminar for the Office of Pesticides and Toxic Substances, U.S. Environmental Protection Agency, May 14, 1980), p. 1.

75. Whelan, "Chemicals and Cancerphobia," p. 8.

76. *House Hearings*, 1981, p. 290.

77. Whelan, "Chemicals and Cancerphobia," p. 8.

78. Gould, Inc., advertisement.

79. *Senate Hearings*, 1968.

80. *Senate Hearings*, 1972, p. 37.

81. Crickmer, "How Much Is Enough?," p. 29.

82. Monsanto, "The Chemical Facts of Life," p. 2.

83. Ibid., p. 13.

84. Ibid.

85. "Must OSHA Make Sense?" *Fortune*, 26 March 1979, p. 32.

86. "OSHA's Crusade," p. 86.

87. *Business Week*, 4 April 1977, p. 74.

88. "If OSHA Is After You," *Nation's Business*, January 1978, p. 56.

89. "OSHA Gets to Work Erasing Unnecessary Regulations," *Nation's Business*, January 1978, p. 16.

90. "OSHA Tries for a Fresh Start," *Business Week*, 3 April 1978, p. 109.

91. The words in this list are not from any single source, but occur throughout the discourse of industry advocates.

92. *Senate Hearings,* 1968, p. 587.

93. Ibid.

94. "Needed: Workers' Compensation," AFL-CIO *Viewpoint.*

95. "Medical Exams Are First Weapon In Protecting You In The Workplace," *The Chemical Worker,* September 1982, p. 9.

96. *Labor Occupational Health Program Monitor,* July 1982, p. 1.

97. *Senate Hearings,* 1972, p. 294.

98. Stansbury, "The Battle For Workplace Safety," p. 13.

99. Vernon M. Jensen, Oil, Chemical, and Atomic Workers Local 8-891, *House Hearings,* 1981, p. 133.

100. See, for example, *House Hearings,* 1981, pp. 54, 132-133.

101. Seidenstein, "Landmark Case on Asbestos."

102. "How To Crack the Company's Code: Getting Names of Workplace Chemicals," United Auto Workers *Occupational Safety and Health Newsletter,* December 1977, in *House Hearings,* 1981, p. 655.

103. *House Hearings,* 1981, p. 52.

104. Ibid.

105. Nolan W. Hancock, Oil, Chemical and Atomic Workers, *House Hearings,* 1981, p. 102.

106. Joanna Brown and Ronni Scheier, "Workplace May Be Hazardous to Health of Blue Collar Minorities," *The Chicago Reporter,* March 1981, in *House Hearings,* 1981, p. 28.

107. Ibid., p. 32.

108. See, for example, *House Hearings,* 1981, p. 251.

109. Ibid., p. 111.

110. Ibid., p. 134.

111. Ibid., p. 876.

112. Stansbury, "The Battle For Workplace Safety."

113. For a discussion of the tension between rights and economic costs, see Kelman, "Occupational Safety and Health Administration," pp. 265-266.

114. See, for example, Tucker, "If We've Done So Much," p. 7, and *Senate Hearings,* 1972, p. 276.

2

DISPUTED KNOWLEDGE:
WORKER ACCESS TO HAZARD INFORMATION

Michael S. Brown

Conflict over health hazards at work is expressed in a variety of ways. On the shop floor workers vie with management over conditions that may cause exposure to toxic substances. In bargaining sessions employers and unions negotiate contract language requiring the provision and maintenance of a safe workplace. In legislative and agency proceedings adversaries contest the development of laws and regulations that would mandate changes in the work environment. At each level these conflicts invoke questions about workers' access to risk information.

There is little agreement on what workers should know, who should provide them with information, and how they should be informed. Disagreements follow from differing views of the problems created by hazardous substances. Citing cases of employer callousness toward worker health and safety in testimony at public hearings, workers contend that employers rarely tell them about hazards or identify the chemicals used in the workplace. Access to such information is crucial to the ability of workers to take adequate precautions, to seek appropriate medical care, and to influence working conditions.

Representatives from industry disagree, arguing that workers need not know the specific chemical identity of a substance to take proper precautions. Knowing which hazards are present, how to prevent exposure, and what to do in emergencies is adequate.

Disagreements over worker access to hazard information take place in a context of a rapidly changing set of laws and regulations governing employer disclosure policies. Yet legal requirements do not necessarily match the realities of the shop floor. After setting the context of occupational health disputes, I will review the legal basis of disclosure policies. Then, through a series of case studies, I will suggest the effects of conflict over access to information on the efforts of workers to become better informed about the risks of their jobs.

THE ADVERSARIAL CONTEXT
OF OCCUPATIONAL HEALTH DISPUTES

Industry is hardly monolithic in its actions regarding risks. The size of the firm and the nature of the production process shape perspectives and policies toward risk. Yet most firms face competitive pressures and customer or client demands that place a premium on reducing production costs. Health and safety expenditures tend to increase capital and labor costs while slowing production, leaving managers with difficult planning choices. Diverting resources to health and safety can adversely affect profits, especially in an environment in which competitors do not make similar investments. If a firm can externalize the costs of occupational illnesses through avoiding payment of compensation or replacing workers, it makes little economic sense to invest in costly measures that protect the health of employees. Thus, there are few economic incentives to improve workplace conditions.

The organizational structure of firms further limits promotion of health and safety. Managers with the authority to make investment decisions are quite removed from the day-to-day operations. Line supervisors who are familiar with conditions are responsible for production and evaluated on their ability to maintain productivity. Communicating information about hazards may lead to worker concerns and complaints, thereby reducing productivity. There is little incentive to openly discuss health and safety problems.

Workers are concerned primarily with wages, benefits, and job security. Although obviously preferring not to become sick or disabled, those with few alternatives usually will endure dangerous conditions to meet their financial obligations. Those few who actively try to force management to clean up the workplace may be harassed by employers and ostracized by coworkers if their efforts threaten job security. Vulnerable to economic pressures, workers often avoid expressing their worries or even seeking information about toxic substances.

Although unions currently represent only 20% of the nation's labor force, they have had a substantial effect on occupational health policies. Using federal grants to hire technical staff, generate educational materials, and train local and regional safety representatives, many unions provide hazard information to their members. Their influence also may extend to nonunion workers through their role in organizing local committees on occupational health[1] and lobbying for more stringent laws and regulations. Unions are divided into local shops with direct contact with members. The national offices perform coordinating and general policy-setting roles.[2] Backed by the resources of the national staff, local officers are responsible for resolving day-to-day problems, including health and safety, and particularly for providing information.

Advocates of workers' right to know about hazards contend that information about exposures, health records, toxic effects, legal rights, emergency measures, and protective actions should be available in all situations. They rest their claims on utilitarian, political, and ethical grounds. For example, they argue that hazard information is necessary to protect themselves and coworkers. Only with sound knowledge are workers able to recognize danger, decide whether or not to accept a hazardous assignment, and protect themselves. Ignorant workers are likely to be complacent and, therefore, at greater risk. Information also is useful in seeking medical care and compensation for work-related illnesses. Activists also argue that information is politically important, for only knowledgeable workers can participate effectively in policy decisions.

Finally, it is argued that individuals have a right to make informed decisions about risks. Much like patients faced with choices among therapeutic alternatives, workers should have adequate information about the risks of an assignment and alternatives in order to give their informed consent before accepting dangerous jobs.

The prevailing industrial perspective is that workers need only know what substances in the workplace are dangerous and, most important, how to work safely. This view reflects the assumption that management acts responsibly to evaluate hazards and to reduce exposures and that residual risks can be attributed to carelessness. Seeking to minimize complaints and avoid reluctance to handle dangerous materials, management has a stake in limiting the communication of detailed information in sensitive areas. Industry is particularly upset if worker or union demands for information jeopardize trade secrecy.

POLICIES, LAWS, AND PROGRAMS

Conflicting perspectives on health and safety are reflected in struggles over legislation and regulations affecting management obligations toward employees and in the educational programs and materials available to workers.

Legal obligations between employers and employees initially developed from the social and economic theories dominating English and American jurisprudence in the nineteenth century.

The belief in laissez-faire capitalism resulted in minimal legal obligations on the part of employers to protect the health of their employees:

> [T]he workman was an entirely free agent . . . expected therefore to accept and take upon himself all of the usual risks of his trade, together with any unusual risks of which he had knowledge, and to relieve his employer of any duty to protect him.[3]

Such beliefs obstructed workers' demands for protection. An engine mechanic in the 1920s related the following experience:

> I asked for one of these Edison fans to be placed in the department . . . to get some ventilation—talk about being called a Bolshevik or Anarchist. The idea of a workingman asking to have a fan . . . to circulate a little current of air where he worked—why it looked like I was a fellow with a great deal of gall. . . . They said I had a lot of guts.[4]

Efforts to educate workers about occupational diseases were rare and often initiated outside the workplace. A booklet put out by the Metropolitan Life Insurance Company in 1913 for workers emphasized the need for an educated workforce and listed basic concepts of industrial hygiene:

> Most industrial diseases are preventable. The bad conditions that exist in factories . . . are due mainly to ignorance. . . . Dangerous conditions continue to exist because neither employer nor employee knows what is going on. They do not understand that dust and fumes, bad air, poor lighting and dirt make sick men and a poor product.[5]

Few specific legal obligations were imposed on employers in this early period. Common law[6] held that employers had "the duty to give warning of dangers of which the employee might reasonably be expected to remain in ignorance."[7] This did not necessarily mean that an employer had to inform workers of hazards. The courts presumed that experience provided adequate knowledge about routine risks.[8] An employer had only to provide warnings for risks that were abnormal or extraordinary. Once informed, employees were assumed to have accepted those risks voluntarily and could not subsequently bring a suit if injured or made ill by the job. Common law obligations to provide adequate warnings were eliminated when states began to adopt workers compensation laws. These laws turned the compensation system into the sole remedy for workplace injuries. Barring lawsuits, they reduced the incentive for employers to inform workers of extraordinary hazards.

Attitudes toward communicating health and safety information to workers remained substantially unchanged until Congress enacted the Occupational Safety and Health Act (OSH Act) in 1970.[9] OSHA did not specifically require employers to provide occupational health programs, but Congress indicated the need for such programs (Section 2(b)(1)) and for joint labor-management efforts to reduce occupational diseases (Section 2(b)(13)). Thus, it directed the secretary of labor to establish training and education programs for employers and employees on hazards and their prevention (Section 21(c)(1)).

OSHA has issued over 100 regulations containing training requirements and, although most refer to safety hazards, a significant number involve toxic substances. Some of these cover specific chemicals, such as asbestos, coke oven emissions, and vinyl chloride. Others involve work processes such as welding, entering confined spaces, and proper respirator use. OSHA also has recommended training guidelines that involve employee participation: Employers, for example, should ask workers about the presence of hazardous conditions and their opinions on existing barriers to knowledge.[10] As a voluntary policy, however, this can be adopted or ignored.

Company medical records also are subject to OSHA rules that allow employees and their designated representatives to read and copy their own records and those of similarly situated employees.[11] The rule, however, does not require companies to generate any records. Employers must provide the generic identity of substances, but they may negotiate confidentiality agreements if trade secrecy is involved.

Stringent requirements for information disclosure have been enacted by over 20 state and local legislatures. Colloquially known as "right-to-know" laws, some simply require making lists available to workers, while others require comprehensive training programs. New York State, for example, allows workers to ask employers for information about toxic substances.[12] Employers must respond with detailed information within 72 hours. If a response is delayed, an employee has the right to refuse to work with the substance until the employer complies with the law. Trade secrets are protected in New York, although hazard information must be communicated if requested. The law also mandates annual training of employees who are exposed regularly to dangerous chemicals.

In some states workers' compensation laws impose an obligation to warn workers about certain hazards. A California court upheld a claim of a worker with an asbestos-related disease, stating that management must inform an employee of any work-related illnesses uncovered during medical examinations.[13] Failure to do so demonstrates a willful intent to do harm.

Following nearly a decade of work on a federal rule providing for employer communication of workplace hazards, OSHA issued its Hazard Communication standard in November 1983.[14] The changes from its initial formulation in the mid-1970s to its final form were substantial, reflecting changes in administrative perspectives toward worker access to information. In 1975 an OSHA Standards Advisory Committee advocated a "total systems" approach, including initial and periodic training of workers and the provision of information about biological effects, symptoms, protective gear, emergency procedures, and proper personal hygiene.[15] That year the National Institute for Occupational Safety and Health (NIOSH) also issued a criteria standard for hazardous materials labeling that emphasized the need for labeling all containers and piping with the identity of substances, and for appropriate training and education programs.[16] Shortly thereafter, OSHA drafted a proposed rule incorporating many of these recommendations, but did not publish it for review and comment.

Under the Carter administration, OSHA proposed a rule that would have identified the chemical name of all substances in all workplaces and allowed employees access to trade secrets.[17] Immediately after taking office, the Reagan Administration withdrew the proposal and reissued it as a Hazard Communication Standard.[18] The new proposal allowed for wide employer discretion in determining existing hazards, did not require disclosure of trade secrets, and was limited to manufacturing employers. The final rule, based on the proposal, is due to go into effect by May of 1986. Designed to supercede state and local statutes, it requires chemical manufacturers and importers to assess the hazards of chemicals that they produce or import, and manufacturing employers to provide training and education on hazardous substances, including their effects, emergency measures, and proper handling procedures. The rule is very flexible, however, allowing an employer to determine what hazards should trigger the new requirements. It grants physicians and health professionals access to trade secret information, but does not allow workers the right to specific chemical names.

Industry likes the new rule, believing it is workable and will provide needed uniformity across the country. In contrast, organized labor is disturbed, because the OSHA rule is weaker than most state and local laws. Unions are irritated that workers would not have access to trade secrets, arguing that they must know the generic identity to evaluate their employers' hazard determinations. Several unions along with three states have sued OSHA, hoping to overturn the preemption of state and local laws.[19]

These policy differences in the approach toward the information about health and safety that should be available to workers are reflected in the educational programs offered by employers on the one hand and unions on the other. To illustrate these differences, let us compare two health and safety programs, one developed by the National Paint and Coatings Association (NPCA),[20] a trade association of paint manufacturers, and another by the United Brotherhood of Carpenters and Joiners of America (UBC).[21]

NPCA has created an animated audio-visual program to explain its hazard identification system for paint manufacture. Using simple language and "cartoon" situations, the program emphasizes workers' responsibility for following the procedures established by management. It briefly mentions alternative methods of controlling exposures, but focuses on what workers should do to protect themselves. The system rates each substance according to its hazard and then cross references the hazards with proper personal protection equipment. It is assumed that management has properly evaluated the hazards and offered adequate protection. Workers have little, if any, role to play in the identification and control of exposures, other than to wear the proper equipment.

In contrast, the carpenters' audio-visual program emphasizes the employer's responsibility for providing a safe workplace. Slides of UBC members at work are combined with narration explaining hazards and describing workers' experiences. The program covers a range of issues: the legal rights of workers, the possibility of engineering controls, and the nature of chronic hazards. The union's health and safety staff offers a full program of training over a three-day period and shorter sessions for those who want an overview of health and safety concerns.

The two training programs differ both in content and attitude. The management program focuses on the hazard identification system. Using the hazard ratings, workers should be able to follow proper procedures. NPCA assumes that management has identified all hazards and, if employees are careful, risks will be minimal. The UBC program suggests that proper procedures are necessary, but workers should be vigilant in identifying hazardous conditions. Moreover, UBC suggests that workers seek engineering controls or safer substitutes, rather than relying only on protective gear. From the union, workers get the message that management may not make health and safety decisions in their best interests, and that workers themselves must participate in the control of risk.

CASE STUDIES

In the political and legal context described above, what happens when workers try to become informed about the hazards of their jobs? How, in fact, do workers acquire information about chemicals in the workplace? The following cases are based on extensive interviews with people who were exposed to chemicals at work.[22] Each case focuses on the experience of a worker in a particular occupational setting. The individual was selected because he or she clearly expressed the experiences of those who worked in that setting. The cases demonstrate differences in workers' approaches to acquiring hazard information, responses by employers, and the usefulness of various laws and regulations.

Case 1: Blueprint and Photo Laboratory

Mike was a film processor in a family-owned, nonunion blueprint and photography laboratory with 15 other employees. His job involved darkroom work, making contact prints and blueprint and mylar reproductions. He spent most of his time running a film processor, filling it with the proper chemicals, and fixing minor breakdowns. Mike handled a variety of toxic chemicals, including film developers and fixers. Because the darkroom had to be light-tight and free of dust—the room had an air conditioning and heating unit operating on positive pressure—ventilation was a problem. Unfortunately, the lack of intake ducts allowed vapors from a developer replenishment system to pollute the air. Occasional ammonia leaks exacerbated the air quality problem. Mike noticed that if he spilled the chemicals on his clothes and did not clean them quickly, holes developed. Other chemicals turned his hands yellow and disintegrated the fingers of his rubber gloves. He also experienced some respiratory difficulties that he suspected were related to chemical exposures. Several employees had complained of disorientation, respiratory congestion, and flu-like symptoms that they attributed to their working conditions.

Some of the chemicals had warning labels that advised users to avoid skin and respiratory contact. Mike asked his supervisor for more information, and asked a friend to contact several manufacturers for their hazard data. He also went to his doctor about his symptoms. Management did not respond to Mike's request for information. Rather, they denied that toxic substances were present in the work environment. At the time of the interview, he had received only a few responses from manufacturers about hazards. His doctor knew little about occupational illnesses.

Mike believed that the problem was in the ventilation system and he confronted management on this issue. His activism extended to calling OSHA and participating in a union-organizing drive. This effort brought little change in working conditions. He attributed his limited success both to attitudes of management and to his coworkers' perceptions of the consequences of activism. Mike was single and had few financial burdens. Other workers with family and financial responsibilities were nervous that activism would jeopardize their jobs in a period of rising unemployment. They also lacked interest in seeking information about hazards because they felt they could do little about them.

Case 2: Electronics Factory

James was an assembler-tester in a large electronics factory that employed about 10,000 people and dominated the economic life of the surrounding small industrial city. The company was nonunion, but a few employees, including James, were trying to organize the plant. The company, known as paternalistic, vigorously opposed their organizing efforts. James encountered a variety of health hazards on the job. The ink used in the printing machines he assembled decomposed into benzene (a carcinogen) and other compounds. The company changed the ink, but did not identify the new substance. Other substances used in the plant included methyl chloroform, freon, epoxies, asbestos, trichloroethylene, perchloroethylene, and PCBs from capacitors broken in the process of tearing down old computers. James heard anecdotal reports of a high rate of miscarriages among women working on the silicon chip line who were exposed to perchloroethylene and lead fumes.

James believed that management deliberately limited information about such risks and expected workers to be satisfied with the information they provided. Management, in his view, wanted complacent workers who were not likely to disrupt production. The company argued that they kept workers informed of the significant hazards through training and chemical precaution sheets (MSDSs). Workers, indeed, could ask for MSDSs on most substances encountered on the job, but James felt they were inadequate for his needs because they often were incomplete and much of the information was incomprehensible.

The company did not offer much chemical safety training. In his nine years on the job, James had attended one company-sponsored training course that consisted of a British film with no particular relevance to his factory. Workers were not told that the government regulated toxic substances or how to determine if they were overexposed to a toxic chemical. If employees wanted more information, they had to be discreet. Concerned about the reportedly high rate of miscarriages, James and others tried to contact the women working on the silicon chip line to identify the extent of the problem. However, when a supervisor learned about James's inquiries, he was called into the manager's office and told to stop asking questions.

A company engineer told James about the change in printer inks and the possibility that the new ink might be mutagenic. The MSDS identified the substance only by trade name, making it impossible to consult other sources for more information. He considered filing a request for further information under the state right-to-know law, but decided against it out of fear of losing his job.

James also asked the company doctor for his medical and exposure records, his right according to OSHA's Records Access rule. He wanted to identify the substances to which he had been exposed and the extent of his exposure during his nine years of employment. James was disappointed with the summary because it did not indicate any exposures. When he asked the doctor to start recording exposure levels, the physician said that he had never encountered any occupationally related diseases in his 35 years at the plant.

Several workers, including James, began an organizing and information campaign. Circulating leaflets, they tried to interest coworkers in health and safety and other concerns. They also tried to enlist the local news media. James believed that the company made few improvements as a result of worker actions and consistently denied any connection between work and health. Furthermore, they treated activists as trouble makers, keeping extensive records on them.

Although a few workers were interested in challenging management, most of James's coworkers did not believe that exposure to toxic chemicals was a serious problem. They felt their employer would not deliberately expose them to harm and saw no need for hazard information. Several factors explain the relative quiescence of the workforce. First, chemical hazards were a recent problem in the plant. Prior to the late 1960s, most of the work involved mechanical assembly of machine parts. The silicon chip production line and the intensive use of degreasers and solvents were relatively new job assignments. Older workers resisted viewing chemicals as hazardous and were concerned more about routine safety problems. Second, the company sought to maintain control by providing decent wages and benefits and threatening to shift production work to another plant. The dominant position of the company in the local economy made workers reluctant to jeopardize well-paying, seemingly secure jobs. Finally, the company's paternalistic style encouraged workers to defer to the judgment of management in the belief that they always acted in the employees' best interests.

Case 3: Art Museum

Jocelyn was a secretary at a museum on a college campus. The museum employed over 30 people, including technical and clerical staff, maintenance workers (who were represented by a union), and administrators. The collection was housed in a modern building that was tightly insulated and climate-controlled to protect the artwork. Shortly after Jocelyn began working there, she suffered from dizzy spells, skin and eye irritation, and gynecological problems. Other employees reported similar symptoms.

Several workers brought their symptoms to the attention of their supervisors and asked if there were any chemicals that might be causing their problems. Management's health and safety department investigated conditions and sought to reassure employees that hazards did not exist. Workers were told to keep quiet while the department investigated the situation. Then, during a reaccreditation visit, an investigator found an oily deposit on the paintings that a laboratory identified as diethylamino ethanol (DEAE), a chemical added to the humidifying system to prevent corrosion. A clerical employee responsible for opening the museum's mail discovered a memorandum about DEAE, stating that a higher level of the substance was present than was allowed by OSHA and that the substance was a skin and eye irritant. Suspecting that this might be a source of workers' symptoms, Jocelyn informally surveyed the illnesses among her coworkers. She found that at least half of the workers reported symptoms including eye damage, skin rashes, gynecological problems, and respiratory irritation. She also went to a doctor, who told her that he thought a chemical had splashed into her eyes, although an opthalmologist refused to make a definitive diagnosis.

During the next year, the workers (through the union representing the maintenance workers) filed a right-to-know request asking management for more information about the toxic effects of DEAE and about exposure levels. Management brought in an outside firm to evaluate the situation, but did not release the results. However, the building superintendent, sympathizing with the workers and defying orders, shut down the air circulation system and opened the external doors while waiting for the system to be fixed. Meanwhile, management argued that the DEAE was getting into the museum air because of clogged filter traps that, if cleaned, would solve the problem. In any case, according to management, the substance was only mildly toxic.

The workers asked the union representing the maintenance employees to request a Health Hazard Evaluation from NIOSH to determine the extent of the problem.[23] NIOSH conducted its evaluation about six months after the workers' initial request and expected to release a final report about one year after its inspection. A preliminary report confirmed the presence of DEAE in the museum and suggested that the substance had permeated the porous fabrics covering the walls and nonporous surfaces. NIOSH agreed with management's assessment of toxicity, but recommended a thorough cleaning of the building and all inside surfaces. The administration proceeded with the cleaning and replaced the defective humidifying system.

Jocelyn and her coworkers were aggressive in searching for information. Distrust of management led to their use of a wide range of sources. They were vocal about the problem both in the workplace and in local newspapers. There was substantial group solidarity about the need for action, probably due to the large percentage of workers who reported problems (over 40% in Jocelyn's survey). Yet uncertainty over whether or not their ailments were job-related made it difficult to maintain unified support for demands. Jocelyn ascribed their successes to publicity and to divisions of opinion within management. The museum director initially supported the workers' point of view, which helped them to win some of their demands. However, when the central administration responsible for implementing museum policies opposed their requests, they made little headway. Even so, she gained greater management cooperation than did either Mike or James.

Case 4: Plant Research Facility

Sheila worked as a laboratory technician in a research institute on biological control of agricultural pests. The workforce was nonunion and included scientists, technicians, and graduate students. Each laboratory was managed independently by the principal scientific investigator. Technicians worked on pesticides and biological agents, both potentially hazardous to human health. Large quantities of laboratory chemicals, including radioactive materials, were stored and used for experiments. Sheila reported having problems with fungus spores, hydrogen sulfide, benzene, ether, and xylene. During her two years on the job, her lung function becamed impaired and she felt ill much of the time. Other technicians told of suffering from dizziness, headaches, blurred vision, and respiratory and skin irritations.

After working in the laboratory for several months and suffering from minor symptoms, Sheila asked her supervisor (who was chair of the safety committee) for information about the chemicals and fungi used in her experiments. She wanted to know about available protective measures. Little information was forthcoming from supervisory personnel, most of whom did not know the toxicological properties of chemicals or refused to believe that there were risks. Her supervisor told her that the fungus with which she worked had been tested on animals with no ill effects. However, researching the scientific literature, she found that the tests involved direct injection of the fungus into body organs, rather than inhalation, which was her own route of exposure. In response, her boss suggested wearing a surgical mask, which she did; but she later discovered that the spores were smaller than the pores of the mask, rendering it ineffective. Her informal investigations led her to believe that a design fault in the ventilation ducts were a source of problems; the exhaust ports were near intake vents that recycled polluted air through the laboratories. In addition, the filters were too small for the ducts, yet still met the design specifications. As a consequence, air flow was not properly controlled.

Sheila asked the safety committee if she could distribute a health questionnaire to the technicians and scientists in the building. The safety committee refused, stating that the questionnaire was biased and could cause mass hysteria. Nevertheless, her interest in health and safety prompted coworkers to tell her their complaints and she began to investigate them. Sheila would track down the source of exposure, identify the chemical, and look up the hazard in reference materials available at the institute. Her biggest need was for information about exposure levels and strategies to improve conditions. She called the county health department and was told that they were unable to help her because the laboratory was not in their jurisdiction. She then filed an OSHA complaint, which resulted in several inspections. The quality of the inspections led to bitter complaints: On one visit OSHA officials did not bring the proper monitoring equipment; during another technicians were not doing the work that generated the problem. When the workers offered to recreate the suspected conditions, OSHA refused to participate, stating that it was an artificial situation. Consequently, exposure levels were never accurately measured. Armed with a petition signed by nearly every employee, the technicians asked for a health and safety training program. Management refused and issued a memorandum stating that workers should use common sense when working with chemicals.

Complacency about chemical hazards was widespread among scientists at the institute, who felt little need for information about toxicity. Many considered themselves to be adequately informed as a result of their training and experience in chemistry and biology. Few realized that such experience was not equivalent to expertise in toxicology. In Sheila's view, they understood chemical reactions but not the effects of chemicals on humans. The laboratory technicians, in contrast, had mixed attitudes toward the hazards of research. Many identified with the goals of the research and felt that the hazards were justified in the pursuit of scientific achievement. Still, they complained about noxious fumes and willingly signed the petition for a training program. Sheila, hardly complacent, served as an information source. When management failed to respond adequately to her inquiries, she did her own research and sought information from experts outside the institute. Later, Sheila and several other activists left the laboratory. The other technicians became relatively quiescent, finding it easier to ignore hazards than to make demands on management. This suggests the important role played by those who are willing to seek information.

Case 5: Pharmaceutical Plant

Laura was a filter cleaner in a large pharmaceutical plant owned by a multinational corporation. Of the 3500 people making and testing drugs and vitamins, over 1000 were union members. The employees mixed raw materials, compressed them into the required form, filled and packaged the drugs, and did maintenance work and laboratory tests. The company made over 100 drugs and vitamins using hundreds of chemical substances. Processing generated significant dust levels that created problems for operators and maintenance workers like Laura. Nosebleeds, respiratory irritation, and bronchitis were common complaints. Maintenance workers were exposed to unknown combinations of substances when changing filters. Two of the drugs that were of great concern to workers were methotrexate, a chemotherapeutic agent, and acetazolamide, a diuretic. The company banned fertile women from working with either drug because of their potential fetotoxicity.

In response to a union right-to-know request, the company gave the union a computer listing of all substances used in the plant and a standard form listing possible adverse effects. Some chemicals were listed only by trade name, but after further union demands, the company provided the generic identities. Distrustful of management, a union official regularly went through the warehouse to see if there were any substances not on the list. The company rarely made exposure data available to workers, nor did it specify exposure limits, only stating that exposures were within legal requirements and less than the recommended therapeutic doses deemed safe by the Food and Drug Administration.[24]

The company prepared MSDSs listing hazards, potential exposures, and precautions for some, but not all, production jobs. These also were given to workers in response to information requests. The company had a brief respiratory protection training program in which workers were told how to use a respirator. Otherwise, safety training was minimal and, according to Laura, considered a farce.

The union local had reference books and articles on toxic substances that Laura and others often used. They also used the extensive health and safety resources of the international to get in-depth information about substances in the plant. For example, the union sent in a medical team to evaluate cancer

rates among workers. Concerns about the effect of male exposure to methotrexate led the union to request testing data held
by the company and to ask OSHA for biological monitoring of
the men working with the material. A year later, the agency still
had not responded.

A safety committee member asked his department to set up a
toxics information program on the materials used in the section. He suggested picking three products and having a meeting at which the company would tell the workers about the
products' uses, adverse reactions, and proper precautions. One
supervisor, a registered pharmacist, concurred, believing he
had a professional obligation to explain the effects of the
drugs; but the company never instituted the proposed program.

Workers also asked for regular monitoring of exposures,
especially on the night shift when maintenance staff were not
present, to make sure the ventilation system was working properly. The head of the company's safety department assured the
joint safety committee that they constantly were monitoring
the work sites. However, a night shift worker insisted that the
safety people were not available to monitor conditions at night.

Despite the company's reluctance in certain areas, this case
is striking for the relative wealth of information available to the
local union and employees. Activists made numerous requests
for information from management and sought data from
alternative sources, such as COSH groups and health professionals. There was an impressive library of materials at the
local union hall. However, Laura contended that most workers
were not interested in the health and safety materials. She
attributed this to a combination of ignorance and fear that
action would threaten job security.

Case 6: Chemical Plant

Ted worked as a welder for a subsidiary of a large multinational conglomerate. His company made organic chemicals

used in the production of plastics, synthetics, pesticides, and pharmaceuticals. At one time, employment totaled over 250, with about 150 belonging to a union. A recession had resulted in layoffs leaving only 50 bargaining unit employees. Labor-management relations had been cordial until a change in ownership led to a six-month strike primarily over health and safety issues. The experience left many union members with bitter feelings toward the company.

Workers used numerous toxic substances, including cyanide, toluol, ketones, phthalic anhydride, formaldehyde, hydrochloric acid, benzene, and monochloroacetic acid. Some of these are known or suspected carcinogens; others cause central nervous system effects, respiratory problems, and severe skin allergies. People reported work-related symptoms ranging from dermatitis covering their entire body to bone cancer.

Ted's local had one of the strongest collective bargaining agreements on health and safety in the country. The strike had resulted in a contract that guaranteed workers access to the generic identity of all substances used in the workplace and required the company to explain the hazards of production. Every third week, management gave the union an updated list of substances used in the plant. When trade secrets were involved, the union signed an agreement stating that it would use the information only for health and safety purposes. Workers also had a contractual right to their medical and exposure records. Mandatory classroom training for new employees covered safety equipment, awareness of hazards, and use of material safety data sheets. Workers received more training from coworkers when they began their production jobs and had access to a book on hazards in each section of the plant.

During these activities, the company, according to Ted, supplied only the minimum amount of information required by law. All piping, drums, and containers were labeled, but workers complained that the labels had only standard warnings. Unless they looked up the substance in a reference book, they would not be aware of specific toxic effects and precautions. Company training emphasized safety hazards and paid minimal attention to health risks. Even when the company did inform workers of health hazards, Ted observed, "It's like handing a stone-age man a rubber grip for his club. What do I do with it?"

The local union relied on the resources of the international to supplement and extend their knowledge of chemical hazards. When a union industrial hygienist found that workers were exposed to reproductive and carcinogenic hazards, the union had researchers from a major teaching hospital do an epidemiological study. The international union also created a training program for rank-and-file workers. Representatives from Ted's local attended a regional health and safety workshop. Union staff and outside experts provided the workers with basic occupational health information.

Several workers remarked that the most useful information they received came from coworkers who told newcomers about chemicals to avoid, proper procedures, and emergency responses. In addition, the safety committee instructed workers about hazards in the plant. Although not all rank-and-file workers were aware of the hazards, their ignorance apparently was due more to a lack of interest than to any significant barriers to access.

Typically, workers brought problems to the attention of a supervisor or, if necessary, to the union safety committee and higher management. Most minor problems were resolved, but workers felt the company ignored the most significant health hazards and refused to take any blame for conditions. Several workers found that complaints remained unanswered until someone was hurt or killed. Even then, the company blamed accidents on workers' failure to follow proper procedures.

The workers in Ted's plant had significantly greater access to information and power to affect conditions than in many other workplaces. Their contract required the company to provide extensive training and gave workers a right to see their health and safety records. The union had substantial experience in gathering information on health hazards at work, so that workers were in a good position to stay informed about hazards. Yet Ted and other workers described continuing hazardous conditions. As the markets for the company's products began to tighten and layoffs occurred, it became increasingly difficult to maintain rank-and-file interest in health questions. Thus, even an informed workforce could not effectively use its knowledge to change hazardous conditions.

Case 7: Fire Fighting

Bill was a professional fire fighter in a small industrial city and vice-president of the union representing the 180 fire fighters employed by the department. Contract negotiations with the city tended to focus on wage and benefit issues; health and safety rarely were bargaining topics. The fire fighters, obviously accustomed to working in hazardous situations, believed that the benefits of saving lives and property outweighed their personal risks. Besides the mundane risks of heat exhaustion, burns, and collapsing buildings, they faced respiratory and skin contact with combustion products. Over the last several decades, technological advances have changed these hazards. New materials, such as plastics, synthetics, and other chemical products, have led to new problems. Bill was present at an office building fire that exposed fire fighters to PCB and dioxin contamination. A transformer in the basement of the building short circuited, leaked PCB fluids, and caused a fire. The combustion products, which included dioxin, were released into the air and sent through the ventilation system of the building. Bill, along with several companies of fire fighters, was exposed to these chemicals.

Management, prodded by the fire fighters' union, had a long history of concern for safety. Recruits underwent rigorous practical and classroom training, including education on chemical hazards. Bill and other fire fighters considered their training to be thorough and complete, limited only by the interest of the individual and some inadequacies regarding chronic health problems, reflecting more a lack of data than managerial intent to withhold information. The department conducted annual inspections of most of the commercial and industrial sites in the city, so that they would know what to expect if an alarm occurred. The union tried to keep current on national statistics of duty-related injuries and illnesses, and to identify suitable protection methods. A state fire fighters' academy provided training and testing for new equipment.

The fire fighters first found out about the PCB hazard in the office building fire from the electric utility's mechanic, who came to shut off the power. He told them that it was standard practice to destroy contaminated clothes and get a checkup following exposure. Thus, after the fire their clothes and protective gear were buried and they went to the hospital for checkups and blood tests. Their blood samples, however, accidently were destroyed during laboratory analysis before determining their blood levels of PCB or dioxin.

The workers received conflicting reports from doctors and academic sources on the effects of PCB and dioxin exposure. Some said it was harmless, others believed the exposures were very dangerous. Some fire fighters were worried about skin contact, others ignored it.[25] The fire fighters depended on a state health department investigation to provide impartial information, but a reporter uncovered an attempt by state officials to misrepresent the results of laboratory tests performed on air and particle samples from the fire zone. The state told fire fighters that birth rates of chicken embryos were unaffected by exposure to the samples. The reporter found that although birth rates remained the same, birth defects increased dramatically. Between the conflicting opinions of experts and misleading evidence from the state, Bill's coworkers were left confused and anxious.

Although workers were well prepared for fighting fires, they were not well informed about PCB exposure. The aftermath of the office buiding fire revealed problems in the communication process. The union sought information from a variety of sources: personal physicians, other unions, management, health professionals, government agencies, and academics. Individual fire fighters searched for information, but the lack of consensus on effects left them confused and anxious about every pain or headache. Not knowing what their exposures levels had been (because of the destroyed blood samples), they had no idea whether or not they were at risk. Their experiences left them skeptical of experts and public officials. In this case, the positive response of management stands out. The department's administrators identified with the concerns of the rank-and-file and were as irritated as the workers about the problems of getting adequate information after the PCB fire. Solutions, such as wearing masks in a fire zone, were viewed as a joint labor-management responsibility.

ANALYSIS

In all of the above cases workers turned first to management for information about health and safety problems. However, their experiences with this strategy differed. Both Ted (Case 6) and Bill (Case 7) were successful in gaining management's cooperation. Others were able to get some information from their employer, but viewed it as inadequate. Mike (Case 1) had a difficult time getting any information at all.

Several of the cases demonstrate the effect of a strong union organization and rank-and-file interest in more hazard information. Some workers were able to acquire a great deal of information from management. However, typically management was willing to provide information only on health effects, and not on exposure levels. Rank-and-file workers rarely went to the international; they directed their attention to the local's safety committee. Unions were a good source of information, especially when the local union could draw upon extensive health and safety resources from their international union.

Workers had little success in obtaining information from government agencies. Jocelyn (Case 3) found NIOSH uncommunicative and unconvincing. Mike (Case 1), Sheila (Case 4), and Laura (Case 5) all thought that OSHA failed to spot existing hazards and to provide adequate information to workers. Similarly, Bill (Case 7) did not trust state agencies to provide truthful and complete information.

Activists were a primary source of information in several of the cases (especially 3 and 4). Such arrangements were established because of the activists' willingness to listen to coworkers and their desire to confront management. Coworkers who feared the consequences of activism (potential harassment or discrimination) could approach these workers rather than management.

How might current rules and regulations concerning worker access to health and safety information be interpreted and modified in light of the analysis in this chapter? The cases suggest that in the adversarial context of occupational health, policies that merely emphasize improving worker access to health and safety information may not result in a well-informed workforce. Workers who are fearful of job loss or potential discrimination as a result of information-seeking activities are not likely to seek out information about hazards. So, too, workers who believe that conditions cannot be changed even if they are more knowledgeable about job risks will not make extensive use of right-to-know laws and regulations.

These findings suggest a need to review hazard communication policies in the context of a broader analysis of labor-management relations. These policies, reflected in laws, regulations, and programs, emphasize improved worker access to risk information. Most programs rely on worker initiatives. It is primarily unionized workers or activists who take advantage of right-to-know policies. They have little impact on the majority of workers, who are skeptical of the possibilities of changing their situation, face significant barriers to obtaining information due to trade secrecy, or fear reprisals if they make demands. Some workers gain indirectly from the information acquired by activists; but, in general, policies that simply create access without mandatory training fail to reach those they are intended to help.

Set against these findings, OSHA's new Hazard Communication Rule does not appear to be a substantial improvement over existing policies, for it does not address the passivity of most workers. Nor does it address the fundamental lack of trust that underlies the problems of communication. These problems reflect existing relationships on the shop floor. As the cases suggest, workers mistrust the information that comes from management. When employers under the Hazard Communication Rule have the discretion to select those substances subject to disclosure requirements and to determine the content of communication, problems of trust are bound to increase. The failure of the new regulations to specify the means for workers to challenge management's assessment of risk will only breed further mistrust.

More active efforts to disseminate information, however, are unlikely. Information about workplace hazards heightens worker awareness of problematic safety practices and increases conflict. It enables workers to call attention to problems with the quality of working conditions and to make demands that run counter to managerial interests. It is not surprising that information policies are a major source of political contention in the struggle over occupational health.

NOTES

1. See Daniel Berman, *Death on the Job: Occupational Health and Safety Struggles in the United States* (New York: Monthly Review Press, 1981); Charles

Levenstein, Leslie I. Boden, and David H. Wegman, "COSH: A Grass-Roots Public Health Movement," *American Journal of Public Health* 74 (1984): 964-965.

2. Marten Estey, *The Unions: Structure, Development, and Management*, 3rd ed. (New York: Harcourt Brace Jovanovich, 1981).

3. William Prosser, *Handbook on the Law of Torts*, 4th ed. (St. Paul, MN: West Publishers, 1971), p. 526.

4. Workers' Health Bureau, *Proceedings of the First National Labor Health Conference*, Cleveland, June 18-19, 1927 (New York: Workers' Health Bureau of America, 1927), p. 37.

5. C.E.A. Winslow, *The Health of the Worker: Dangers to Health in the Factory and How to Avoid Them* (Metropolitan Life Insurance Company, 1913), p. 3.

6. Common law refers to the development beginning in England and adopted in the United States of judges making law in the absence of statutory language. Common law rests heavily on interpretations of community norms and customs.

7. Prosser, *Law of Torts*, p. 526.

8. Moore v. Morse and Malloy Shoe Co., 89 NH 332, 197 A. 707 (1938); Engelking v. City of Spokane, 49, WA 446, 110 P. 25 (1910).

9. PL 91-596 December 29, 1970.

10. U.S. Department of Labor, Occupational Safety and Health Administration, "Training Guidelines: Request for Comments and Information," *Federal Register*, 30 August 1983, pp. 39317-39322.

11. U.S. Department of Labor, Occupational Safety and Health Administration, "Access to Employee Exposure and Medical Records: Final Rules and Proposed Rulemaking," *Federal Register*, 22 January 1980, pp. 35212-35303.

12. Laws of New York, 1980, Chap. 551.

13. Johns-Manville Products Corp. v. Contra Costa Superior Ct., 612 P.2d 948 (1980).

14. U.S. Department of Labor, Occupational Safety and Health Administration, "Hazard Communication," *Federal Register*, 25 November 1983, pp. 53280-53348.

15. Standards Advisory Committee on Hazardous Materials Labeling, *Report of the Standards Advisory Committee on Hazardous Materials Labeling to the Assistant Secretary of Labor for Occupational Safety and Health, U.S. Department of Labor* (Washington, DC: Government Printing Office, 1975), p. 38. Under Section 7(b) of OSHA, the secretary of labor may establish advisory committees to assist in carrying out the standard-setting functions specified in Section 6.

16. U.S. Department of Health, Education and Welfare, National Institute of Occupational Safety and Health, *Criteria for a Recommended Standard: An Identification System for Occupationally Hazardous Materials*, NIOSH Publication 75-126 (Washington, DC: Government Printing Office, 1975).

17. U.S. Department of Labor, Occupational Safety and Health Administration, "Hazards Identification: Notice of Proposed Rulemaking and Public Hearings," *Federal Register*, 16 January 1981, pp. 4412-4453.

18. U.S. Department of Labor, Occupational Safety and Health Administration, "Hazards Identification," *Federal Register*, 13 February 1981, pp. 12214; "Hazard Communication," *Federal Register*, 19 March 1982, 12092-12124.

19. Bureau of National Affairs, "Three States Join in Steelworker Suit on Hazard Communication; Fourth May File," *Occupational Safety and Health Reporter*, 5

January 1984, pp. 811-812; "OSHA Rule Would Preempt State Laws, Auchter Tells Pennsylvania Senate Group," *Occupational Safety and Health Reporter*, 2 February 1984, p. 948.

20. National Paint and Coating Association, *HMIS Implementation Manual* (Washington, DC: NPCA, 1981).

21. United Brotherhood of Carpenters and Joiners of America, Department of Occupational Safety and Health, *Health and Safety Identification Program* (audio-visual and written materials, n.d.).

22. The cases were derived from interviews conducted between November of 1982 and June of 1983 with people who work (or worked) with or around chemicals. Contacts for interviews were established through labor unions, labor education courses, conferences, and acquaintances. For more detail about the full set of interviews and the specific people involved in the case studies presented here, see Dorothy Nelkin and Michael Brown, *Workers at Risk: Voices from the Workplace* (Chicago: University of Chicago Press, 1984); Michael S. Brown, "The Right To Know: Hazard Information and the Control of Occupational Health" (Ph.D. diss., Cornell University, 1984).

23. The workers decided to go through the union rather than making the request themselves (three people would have had to sign the request form) to avoid disclosure of individuals' names and possible discrimination.

24. A coworker of Laura's felt that the company misrepresented worker exposures as workers were mixing kilograms of product and inhaling the dust while consumers ingested grams.

25. Concern about the risk of dioxin probably was related to Agent Orange. Some of the fire fighters had been in Vietnam (including Bill) and were aware of the Agent Orange controversy.

3

RISK IN THE PRESS:
CONFLICTING JOURNALISTIC IDEOLOGIES

Chris Anne Raymond

In the spring of 1980, Thorne Auchter, the new head of the Occupational Safety and Health Administration (OSHA), appeared in Buffalo, New York for a meeting with local business leaders. During his stay, he agreed to meet some local union representatives at a downtown hotel. The meeting received coverage from the local media as well as from a labor magazine. The accounts were strikingly different—almost as if journalists were writing about two unrelated events.

The coverage in the local morning newspaper, the *Courier Express*, ran under the headline, "OSHA Head Grilled by Unionists." The opening paragraph quoted Auchter as saying, "I don't enjoy surprises." Expecting "half a dozen" people to show up, he faced nearly 200 unionists and environmentalists. Reporter Celia Viggo characterized this audience as "less-than-friendly," packing the room to "roundly denounce his message." The headline of the labor semiweekly, *Solidarity*, differed in tone from the *Courier's*: Labor leaders were the principal focus of attention. Instead of being "grilled," Auchter is confronted:

Author's Note: *This chapter is based on my Ph.D. thesis, "Uncovering Ideology: Occupational Health in the Mainstream and Advocacy Press, 1970-82," Cornell University, Department of Sociology, Ithaca, NY, 1983.*

When OSHA chief Thorne Auchter went to Buffalo to speak to a
business group recently, UAW and other union activists figured they
deserved equal time. So they demanded a meeting, rented a room and
got 150 area unionists together to confront Auchter, who, under the
circumstance, couldn't say no.

Auchter's response was not one of wounded surprise, but of
anger and arrogance:

Auchter, faced with a crowd of over 120, angrily accused [union leader
Tony] Fricano of setting him up. Union members present said he
would have walked out in a huff had not two local TV stations'
cameras been whirring away.

The remainder of the article portrayed Auchter as evasive
and secretive; it placed his appointment to head OSHA under
suspicion, emphasizing that his construction firm had a history
of fines for health and safety violations.

The two accounts of this event had little in common. The
reports differed in tone and emphasis. The *Courier* characterized the unions as inappropriately militant and Auchter as the
concerned official attempting to respond to a union "ambush."
Solidarity portrayed the unions as concerned champions of
democracy, demanding "equal time," and Auchter as an inept,
evasive, image-conscious politician.

Every event has some degree of ambiguity; the more ambiguous and broad-ranging a public issue, the more likely it is that
jounalists will interpret its meaning differently and report it in
differing contexts, shaped by their training and outlook. The
coverage of occupational health in the press is a striking case in
point.

OCCUPATIONAL HEALTH AND NEWS ACCOUNTS

For hundreds of years, occupational disease and industrial
accidents were widely accepted as the inevitable side-effects of

working. The situation changed in the late 1960s, when organized labor made a major push for national legislation. The Occupational Safety and Health Act (OSH Act) was controversial: Business complained of costly and petty regulations; labor complained of lax enforcement and trivial fines. As occupational health became a politically and economically volatile subject, it generated vexing questions: How appropriate and/or effective is government regulation? To what extent are corporations to be held accountable? Are there limits to free enterprise when thousands of workers are unwittingly exposed to hazards? What is the role of scientific expertise? Of organized labor?

These questions are troubling from the standpoint of reporters. Continued technical debates give reporters few guideposts to direct their news coverage, yet the pressing nature of the problem makes it impossible to wait for all the "facts" before writing a story. The efforts of opposing interest groups to define the nature of the problem add to the difficulties in reporting on the topic. Is the occupational health issue to be defined primarily as a scientific/technical issue, a dispute over etiology and appropriate exposure thresholds? As a legal/bureaucratic issue, a controversy over regulatory mechanisms and jurisdiction? As an economic issue, a question of measuring costs and benefits or inflationary impacts? As a political issue, touching on conflicts between capitalism and worker control? As a sociocultural issue, having to do with general values of profit making, efficiency, and attitudes toward work?

Press reports are important in defining the policy agenda, for they often are the only means through which the public is informed. The stakes in their definition are high: If occupational health problems are defined primarily as scientific, money must be invested in the epidemiological and laboratory research necessary to improve understanding. If occupational health problems are defined bureaucratically, policy makers and regulators must answer to an angry public demanding to know why standards are not properly enforced. If the focus is on capitalism and workplace democracy, this raises questions about the very structure of American enterprise and corporate power. Thus, the context and language chosen by journalists for public accounts of occupational health carry assumptions about the nature of the problem and potential solutions.

The following case studies are drawn from two sectors of the press: the *New York Times, Bergen* (New Jersey) *Record,* (Buffalo) *Courier Express, Newsweek,* and *US News and World Report* represent what I will call the "mainstream" press. *In These Times, The Progressive,* and *Mother Jones* are what I call the "advocacy" press. This chapter will make it clear that both press sectors advocate particular political ideologies, but the advocacy press openly acknowledges its ideological stance.[1] The case studies suggest how these ideologies are reflected in news accounts of particular occupational health topics.

In reviewing the coverage of jumpers, the nuclear industry, and DBCP, I will address several questions: In what context is occupational health covered? When is an event covered? What sources are used by the reporter? Who is assumed to have legitimacy as a news source? What metaphors or imagery appear? Following the case studies, I will consider the different working assumptions that emerge from a content analysis of 299 occupational health articles in eight publications and from interviews with journalists.

Case 1: Jumpers

"Jumpers" are nuclear industry workers who undergo brief but intense exposure to radiation in order to repair valves, fix leaks, or clean up spills. As nuclear plants age and maintenance problems increase, jumpers are an important part of the industry's labor force. Industry executives prefer not to use their highly skilled, permanent employees for jobs that would use up their "body bank" of permissible lifetime exposure. Thus, a subsidiary enterprise to recruit temporary workers for maintenance jobs has come into existence.

Sometimes called "sponges," or "stream generator jumpers," jumpers are hired to go into radioactively hot areas of nuclear power plants to make repairs. The jobs generally last no more than a few minutes, but the pay amounts to as much as the workers could earn in two or three weeks elsewhere. The pay is attractive to unemployed, unskilled workers, so the recruitment services have had no trouble attracting people for the job. Estimates of the number of transient workers (as the Nuclear Regulatory Commission calls them) range from 20,000 to 35,000 a year. Less attractive than the salary is the prospect of thousands of Americans receiving doses of radiation in excess of the typical lifetime exposure. This is the point of controversy and the source of media interest.

Jumpers have received markedly different coverage in the mainstream and advocacy press. The only article specifically about jumpers to appear in the *New York Times* (July 1979), "Atom Plants Are Hiring Stand-Ins to Spare Aides the Radiation Risk," focused on the "increasing official concern" among regulatory officials. They were amending record-keeping procedures to require that the industry keep track of their jumpers' cumulative radiation exposure.

Two articles in the advocacy press were *Mother Jones's* "The Glow Boys," an undercover exposé of recruitment practices, and *The Progressive's* "Leap of Faith," an examination of jumpers, the health risks they incur, and the validity of government exposure standards.

The opening paragraphs of the *New York Times* piece offered a vignette of an underemployed folksinger who answered an Atlantic Nuclear Services ad and now has what the article described as a "part-time vocation" and a "career." *Mother Jones*, in contrast, called the job "dying for a living" and a "meat market."

The *Times* noted the criticism of the practice of hiring stand-ins, quoting nuclear expert Karl Morgan of the Georgia Institute of Technology: "The solution is not to hire temporary employees to divide up the dose but rather to correct reactor design failures that are the source of the trouble." The advo-

cacy press also was critical of the practice, but went beyond
that criticism to examine the government's exposure standards
and the structure and motivation of the nuclear industry as a
whole.

The two presses also differ in their coverage of the technical
status of the industry. *Mother Jones* saw jumper recruiting as a
fast-growing business because it is

> an integral part of a bizarre, finger-in-the-dike effort to rescue a
> nuclear industry plagued by chronic and premature mechanical fail-
> ures. Jumpers are part of a work force . . . all recruited in an endless
> cycle like partners in a nonstop cardiopulmonary resuscitation effort.

Although the *Times* noted the increasing number of
jumpers, it did not characterize the problem as inherent to the
entire industry so much as a problem confined to a handful of
companies that have had difficulties at their power plants. Said
Virginia Power's utility director, B. Ralph Sylvia, "When the
(clean-up) project is finished there will be no further need for
the employment of temporary workers of this type."

Yet the recruitment companies keep springing up, a point on
which all the articles agree. Why? What is attracting the
workers? What are they like? Again, there are differences in the
coverage of these questions. For example, the *Times* portrayed
two jumpers: Mike Manto, a folksinger with a part-time vocation as a jumper, and Cynthia White, a mother of two and a
trainer of fellow jumpers. She is quoted:

> It's startling the questions people will ask. They worry about getting
> zapped, about losing their hair, going bald, turning green, going
> sterile. I tell them that I am the same color when I come out of the
> shower as when I go in, I have not turned blue and my sex life is fine.
> The training really helps.

Compare Mrs. White's cheery bravado and Manto's innocuous "career" to the workers portrayed by *The Progressive* and

Mother Jones. There are the urban kids recruited for West Valley, New York clean-up duty. Former Nuclear Fuel Services lab supervisor David Pyles said in *Mother Jones*:

> What a gas for inner-city kids. They had no idea what they were in for, sitting around the lunchroom and getting paid. If they asked about risks they were told radiation just kills a few blood cells. Some were really afraid. I tried to talk them into going home, but they wanted the money.

There is Syd Holsman, who told the undercover *Mother Jones* reporter, "It's easy to laugh when you know you're gonna die," and then adds, after a second thought, "Money is money. I've got a family to support."

There are the workers like Mike Balboa in *The Progressive*, about whom the reporter said:

> For Mike Balboa and others like him who try their hand as jumpers in the nuclear industry, high radiation exposure—with its immeasurable risk to health and life—is the necessary price for the high pay that goes with the job.

Later in the article, Balboa was quoted:

> It was not only the best paying job I could find for the amount of time; it was the only job I could find. I took it without knowing exactly what kind of work I'd be doing.

From the advocacy press's perspective, few workers do know what they are doing when they decide to jump. Their training is described as indoctrination; their trainers are portrayed as sideshow barkers, pulling a fast and slick routine on unsuspecting, desperate men and women. For example, *Mother Jones's* article opened with a training session in which the trainer's talk is described as a "spiel." The writer noted how the trainer modulated his tone of voice to evoke the proper response from workers, how he soothed fear by comparing radiation risks to the danger of handling charcoal briquets, and how he manipulated workers with jokes: "I've always been this short, always been this ugly and I was going bald before I jumped." The trainer is said to sound "like Marlin Perkins of Mutual of Omaha."

The Progressive piece cast a doubtful eye on the enthusiasm of regular nuclear industry employees who sometimes jump, calling them "volunteers" in quotes. The *Times*, on the other hand, said that a call for recruits to help in the Three Mile Island accident "quickly yielded a list of about 100 people" who would not receive extra pay, according to the company, because "this will be at business-as-usual rates, which just points up that those of us who understand radiation are not afraid of it."

In sum, the *New York Times* raised concerns about jumpers in the context of official worry over violations of regulatory policy; the jumpers themselves were shown to be rather unconcerned about their radiation exposure because the job paid well. *Mother Jones* and *The Progressive* had a different perspective: They characterized the jumpers as victims of a bad economy and a deceitful industry, taken in by executives desperate to mend unresolvable design problems by exposing workers to dangerous radiation, and by a regulatory policy only apparently protecting their health.

Case 2: The Nuclear Industry

In addition to the thousands of transient workers, the nuclear industry employs thousands of other workers at all stages of the fuel process from mining to refining and power generation.

The *New York Times* printed fifteen articles on workers in the nuclear industry from 1976 to 1982; the advocacy press carried seven. These figures do not include the Karen Silkwood case or the Three Mile Island accident, because these inherently dramatic events were "automatically" news.

The *Times'* coverage vacillated between articles portraying workers as unconcerned about radiation exposure and articles critical of the industry, particularly after the TMI accident. One article in the fall of 1976, headlined "Atomic Plant Employees Unconcerned Over Perils," reported on the aftermath of a nuclear waste explosion that contaminated several workers. It opened with the assertion that employees take exception to the view "that they skirt disaster in the fiery breath of an atomic dragon." It quoted the president of a group of affiliated unions, who said that his members wish they did not have to drive 40 miles to work—they would rather have the Richland, Washington Hanford Nuclear Reservation "right across the road from home." He had worked at the plant since 1951 and claimed that the only bad part about those years was the boom-town hustle-bustle accompanying the plant's growth.

A woman with a husband and brother working at the Hanford facility recalled an accident back in 1962 that "caused only a sunburn." She argued that working in the plant is no worse than working in a mine, and then asked rhetorically, "how safe is the air-filtering system here in our bank?" A chemical plant operator, employed at the Hanford plant since 1942, told the reporter that he doesn't worry because there is a good safety program. He recalled that he had "a little" radioactive dust on his hands when a glove broke, but it washed off "easier than an inkstain."

A 1977 *Times* article called, "Radiation Overdose: All In A Day's Work," described a worker pulling on his clothes with extra care, then going to work and willingly exposing himself to "the equivalent of 35 chest X-rays to get a water sample." The worker was not concerned about the long-term effects of exposure because he has "100% faith in nuclear power"; in fact, the article said, his greatest concern was to get his children's names in the paper.

Finally, a May 1979 article reporting on government tests of workers unknowingly exposed for 13 years to a radioactive waste dump underneath their factory opened with a vignette of a "robust, 47 year old machine shop operator" reclining in paper pajamas while being tested for whole body radiation. He is bored with the whole thing.

Several *New York Times* articles critical of occupational health in the nuclear industry were pegged to the release of scientific reports; a Health Research Group study of statistics indicating an increase in cancer death rate from presumably safe levels of plutonium exposure; a controversial government study of deaths among atomic workers; and a joint National Academy of Sciences/Department of Energy study of cancer deaths at each stage of nuclear processing. The *Times* articles highlighted the scientific controversies surrounding the research. But instead of delving into the substantive issues of sample size and statistical projection techniques that might lead to an informed evaluation of the research, they reported the charges and counter charges from leading scientific experts. The articles also suggested that such research might "adversely affect the economic viability" of the industry.

The *Times'* coverage of accidental radiation exposures can in some sense be seen as critical of the industry by calling public attention to problems; but the actual treatment of accidents conveys an "all-is-well" image. The *Times* covered four mishaps at nuclear facilities from 1976 to 1982. The first, "Atom Waste Blast Contaminates Ten," reported an explosion at the Hanford Nuclear Reservation in August of 1976. The reporter described the blast and the plant's role as a weapons waste reprocessor, indicating that the explosion was limited in scope and caused only insignificant exposure because the workers left quickly. The company vice president was quoted: "This is the first ever accident like this." In short, the article told us that the accident was an anomaly and not very serious. Several weeks later, however, an Associated Press story appeared, buried next to the sports scoreboard on page 42.

This story reported that the accident was more serious than the original article had suggested; a worker had suffered serious burns, vision problems, internal radiation, and may contract cancer.

A *Times* story from Harrisburg, Pennsylvania headlined "Four Got Overdose of Radiation, But Company Says They're Well," reported that a company spokesman "conceded" that four workers had received overdoses, but that they were unaffected. The reporter noted that none of the workers could be found to confirm reports of their well-being. But the article quoted a vice president at Metropolitan Edison and a utilities licensing engineer, who both downplayed the exposure. A local nuclear medicine physician concurred with this opinion.

Other critical *Times* articles were pegged to bureaucratic/ technical foulups. One of the longest and most critical articles about nuclear workers' health, headlined "Safety Rules Reported Eased to Reopen Nuclear Plant," was about the pressures that plant officials placed on radiation protection staff at the Connecticut Yankee facility during its annual shutdown. Scientific experts and government and company officials observed the "lack of management commitment to health concerns" at the plant and the loss of credibility suffered by health physics personnel as they caved in to pressure to speed up the refueling procedures at the risk of exposing workers to excess radiation. However, utility spokesmen asserted that, despite the poor management, workers did not receive hazardous levels of radiation exposure. The reporter, who interviewed no workers, concluded by noting that the problems had been addressed through "added staff at the corporate level and in the health physics area, improved equipment and training, and overhauled procedures." In other words, the foul-up caused by bureaucratic red tape had been resolved by better bureaucratic practices.

A 1977 feature story, "Cancer Victim's Son Tells of Lost Data," focused on the plight of a man whose father died of cancer, allegedly from entering a highly radioactive silo at a

Department of Energy (DOE) storage facility in Lewistown, New York. Although DOE radiation specialists denied such a possibility, it and ARCO Medical (then in charge of workers' health records) either could not or would not release the father's medical records. The next day's follow-up article, "Energy Agency Asks Data Hunt In Cancer Death," reported that DOE finally had requested ARCO Medical to track down the records; the reporter also noted the increasing concern in the Lewiston community about leaks and higher cancer rates.

The *Times* emphasis on scientific reports and official government and industry sources of information, its portrayal of nuclear radiation as relatively innocuous, and its image of workers as silent and willing participants in the nuclear power industry differed markedly from the coverage given to nuclear power in the advocacy press.

Workers, according to *In These Times, Mother Jones,* and *The Progressive*, are aware of the dangers of work and of lax health and safety practices. Thus, reporters call upon workers themselves as sources of information. A number of articles focus on the primary stage of the nuclear processing cycle—uranium mining. For example, *In These Times* ran a 50-inch article entitled "Navajos Mined Cancer," describing the plight of workers.

Workers and their survivors are quoted extensively about hazardous working conditions. Ray Joe, a 10-year Kerr McGee employee with lung cancer is quoted: "When the driller drilled the ore, they blasted and then they'd go right back in there in the smoke and dust." Widow Mae John, whose husband died of lung cancer after 20 years in the mines, had this recollection:

After the blasting, maybe 10 or 15 minutes later, the men were chased back in there, told to "go back to work." They even used to eat inside the mine, even drink the water dripping inside the mine.

The Progressive's article on uranium mining is similar in tone to *ITT's* piece. Entitled "Bury My Lungs at Red Rock," it ran for four pages in the February 1979 issue. Again, workers and their survivors are quoted about working conditions, contradicting the versions offered by officials in the mainstream press. Again, the government (specifically, the Bureau of Indian Affairs and Atomic Energy Commission) is characterized as a broker for, not a regulator of, big companies. The agencies, the reporter asserted, leased land from the Navajos without regard for adverse environmental and socioeconomic impacts or royalty payments, taking advantage of needy, underdeveloped Indian areas.

> Then, as now, the reservation offered a profitable opportunity for companies like Kerr McGee. On the reservation there were no taxes, little regulation, and cheap labor. "The company came around and said there were many jobs opening up, but they didn't tell us a thing about the dangers of uranium mining," former miner Terry Light recalls. "The labor came cheap back then. The white men really took advantage of the Navajos who needed jobs."

The Nuclear Regulatory Commission characterizes uranium mining and milling as the most significant sources of radiation exposure to the public from the entire uranium fuel cycle, including power plants and high-level radioactive waste sites. Yet the only *Times* coverage was a brief report pegged to an OCAW/Public Health Research Group petition in April of 1980, urging the Labor Department to issue an emergency standard to lower exposure in the mines—a bureaucratic event.

Case 3: DBCP—Disaster or Corporate Crime?

1,3-dibromochloropropane is a chemical widely used in agriculture to control worms attacking fruits, vegetables, cotton, and home garden plants. Approximately 30 million pounds a year were produced in the United States during the mid-1970s, until it was discovered that workers at an Occidental Chemical Company (Oxy) plant in Lathrop, California were suffering from sterility. The news broke in the summer of 1977, when another major producer of DBCP, Dow Chemical, halted production of the pesticide at its plants due to preliminary evidence of sterility or low sperm counts among its workers.

Two different scenarios appeared in the mainstream and advocacy presses. The *New York Times* carried six staff and eleven brief wire service stories from mid-August 1977 to October 1981; *Newsweek* ran a one-page article in August 1977. Their coverage portrayed the DBCP case as a sudden, unexplained, and unforeseeable disaster. No one was to blame; in the words of an Oxy worker quoted in the *Times*:

> Today Mr. Bricker, who has two children, blames himself in part for not pursuing the matter (his and others' sterility), instead of just talking about it. He gets angry when he thinks of the situation. Some of his co-workers, he confirms, are thinking about lawsuits. But, he adds, "Who are you going to blame?"

Although a number of *New York Times* stories and the *Newsweek* article mentioned that earlier studies of DBCP indicated its sterility-causing potential in laboratory rats, this information comes at the end of the articles. Greater emphasis is given to the sudden discovery scenario:

> *Then one day* at lunch in the cafeteria of the Occidental Chemical Company, in Lathrop, Calif., Boss discovered that a number of his colleagues in the pesticide division where he worked were having the same problem (Newsweek lead, emphasis added).

> *Finally, this summer,* six of the section's workers decided to seek fertility tests. . . . *At that point,* DBCP became the villain. . . . *In recent*

days, as people have learned that DBCP is linked not only to sterility, but also to cancer, the problem assumed nationwide dimensions (Opening paragraph, Times, emphasis added).

Once the discovery was made, government and industry were shown responding promptly and judiciously: Oxy and Dow sent out recall notices nationwide and to other countries; they stopped production and sales. The Labor Department issued an emergency standard, began further tests, and expanded the search for hazards to the related pesticide EDB. In a story about the recall notices, the *Times* quoted a Dow spokesman: "We're trying to get on the far side of playing it safe." In another story, called "Sterility Linked to Pesticide Spurs Fear on Chemical Use," the reporter observed:

> Authorities in both industry and government agree that, in the rush to market chemical products after World War II, thousands of substances found their way into use on the basis of tests that by today's standards were inadequate to fully protect the public and the environment. Both industry and Government are now going back in a grim game of catch-up to recheck those chemicals.

Similarly, *Newsweek* reported as follows:

> Since the sterility factor was established, Federal officials have sent telegrams to manufacturers of DBCP to warn them of the danger and advise that workers henceforth be thoroughly protected. Dow... and Shell, which manufacture most of the nation's DBCP, quickly suspended both the production and sale of the chemical.

The *Times* coverage expanded beyond the occupational health angle as the EPA got involved. The first major article carried in the *Times* described the DBCP revelation as "one of the most dramatic, clear-cut and widespread instances of *environmental* contamination since public attention began focusing on such matters in the 1960s" (emphasis added). Yet the story was not principally about general environmental contamination so much as about workers. Subsequent coverage from the wires focused increasingly on the extraoccupational dangers, including articles in June 1979 and October 1981 reporting on drinking water contamination in Visalia, California and an EPA judge's decision to ban the use of DBCP on crops for fear of consumer exposure.

The advocacy's press coverage of DBCP did not expand to broader environmental issues—*ITT's* and *Mother Jones's* four articles focused entirely on pesticide workers. Unlike the discovery-response scenario highlighted in the *Times* and *Newsweek*, the articles in the advocacy press emphasized negligence, exploitation, and official inertia, They also highlighted the active role of unions, the workers' conflicting feelings, and broader structural issues concerning the role of agribusiness and the need for worker control and corporate accountability.

ITT's first article, from the alternative press Liberation News Service, was headlined "Workers Sterilized In Chemical Plant." The lead compared the DBCP event with the 1976 Phosvel scandal—the discovery that Texas pesticide workers suffered profound neurological disorders after exposure to letophos. ITT described the DBCP case as "the latest horror story" and pointed out:

> As far back as 1961, Dow chemical, one of two major producers of the chemical, conducted tests that showed that DBCP affected the reproductive systems of animals. In three species of animals, the drug caused degeneration of the testicles and low sperm count.

Dow and the other companies did not "get on the far side of playing it safe" in this account. Workers at Oxy never were informed of the dangers of the chemical they were handling, says Rafael Moure, an industrial hygienist with OCAW. "The company denied it was a problem," Moure said. "They said workers always wanted to complain about something."

Whereas the mainstream press reported on quick official actions, the advocacy press criticized government and industry inertia:

The man at the California State Health Department made sympathetic clucking noises and said that there was absolutely no way he could prove anything—too many symptoms to cross-check against too many chemicals. "Not enough meaningful research data has been compiled to permit rigorous analysis, you understand?" (Mother Jones, May 1979).

Later, this article—a lengthy review of the activities surrounding the documentary film "The Song of the Canary"— quotes a comment in the film made by Oxy's company doctor: "I've talked to two scientists who are familiar with the work and they both say, 'Heck, we just didn't draw the conclusion that there'd be sterility from the fact that the testicles were shriveling up.' " The journalist asked a rhetorical question:

Well, heck and doubleheck, what's a poor chemical company to do? And what about...OSHA? The film's interviews with OSHA officials evoke the image of a row of ants diligently moving crumbs from Pile A to Pile B, while a huge feast looms all around them, totally beyond their engineering capacity.

The advocacy press articles recounted the DBCP revelations from the point of view of the workers, and they stressed the necessity for union solidarity on occupational health issues:

An active union local or safety committee within the plant or a local organization focusing on health and safety is a vital ingredient to developing momentum around occupational health and overcoming cynicism, confusion and despair.

Whereas the mainstream press focused on the impact of the revelation on official policies, the advocacy press gave greater space to the direct effects on workers' mental and physical health:

They are big men, into muscle shirts, Peterbilt caps and physical boisterousness. On the basis of their size and vigor alone, they seem healthy. They are not. Their noses bleed inexplicably. Some of them can no longer smell at all. Headaches and nausea are facts of their daily lives. Spots appear on their bodies. Some never have children (Mother Jones, May 1979).

Finally, rather than placing the issue in a narrow context of technical and scientific uncertainty and tragic revelation, the advocacy press situated the DBCP case in a broader political and economic context. *In These Times* quoted filmmaker Josh Hanig:

> Workers understand perfectly well what makes the economic system tick. They know their health is, in effect, a line in the budget just like equipment, just like advertising, just part of the competitive balance.

Mother Jones went further in its social analysis. It recounted the accusations of racial and corporate exploitation at the California Department of Food and Agriculture made by Ralph Lightstone, an attorney for California Rural Legal Assistance. It quoted social scientist and former union activist, Stanley Arnowitz:

> The question of occupational health is the question of worker control. No issue raises a greater challenge to the managerial prerogative, a greater challenge to capitalism.

CONTRASTING COVERAGE

The coverage of jumpers, the nuclear industry, and the DBCP story illustrates a number of differences in perspective in the mainstream and advocacy press—differences in the characterization of business, government, and labor; in the legitimacy granted to news sources; in the priorities assigned to occupational and environmental dangers; and in the broader context in which to consider occupational health.

To what degree are these differences reflected in the general coverage of occupational health in the two types of press? How much coverage does the topic receive, and what themes, news sources, and contexts recur?

HOW MUCH COVERAGE?

Analysis of articles in journalistic reviews,[2] and interviews with reporters suggest that coverage of occupational health and safety issues is relatively sparse. This impressionistic evidence is substantiated by a quantitative analysis of coverage in the publications in this sample (*New York Times, U.S. News and World Report, Bergen Record, Courier Express, The Progressive, Mother Jones,* and *In These Times*). Neither press sector devoted large amounts of space to occupational health; in the advocacy press, however, coverage of these issues was significantly greater than in the mainstream press.

The number of articles on occupational health and safety between 1970 and 1982 totals 299. The percentage of total news hole (total editorial space, excluding advertising) given to occupational health over the 12-year period is minimal: none of the publications devoted more than about 3% of its available editorial space to the subject. However, the advocacy press devoted more space to news and analysis of occupational health and safety (see Table 3.1).

In interviews, several mainstream reporters alluded to the way occupational health tended to get lost in the daily or weekly news routine: "It falls in the cracks a lot of times." Some reporters speculated about why occupational health was or was not covered by their publications. Robert Cunningham, Washington bureau reporter for the metropolitan daily in Hackensack, New Jersey, the *Bergen Record*, stated as follows:

[Our coverage was] better than most, I think, About 6-7 years ago, we discovered cancer. Anything to do with carcinogens got a lot of play.

TABLE 3.1

Percentage of Newshole Devoted to Articles about
Occupational Health in Mainstream and Advocacy Press

Publication	Percentage of Space
Mainstream	
New York Times	.24
Bergen Record	.50
Courier Express	.50
Newsweek	1.10
U. S. News	2.50
Advocacy	
Mother Jones	3.20
The Progressive	2.80
In These Times	2.20

NOTE: A t-test of the percentage of newshole the mainstream and advocacy press devote to occupational health shows the differences to be statistically significant. $Z = 5.07$; $p < .005$; d.f. = 7.

To the extent that occupational health stories were about cancer, they got covered, whether they had a real lot to do with it or not. But we've been tailing off. Some of the shock value has worn off.

A fellow reporter admitted that occupational health stories sometimes escaped attention, but avowed that, "the good story always gets out somehow."

Does it? Certainly the *Chicago Sun-Times*, the *Bergen Record*, and the *Los Angeles Times* have done excellent series on occupational health hazards pegged to particular hazardous industries in their regions. But these seem to be exceptions to the general state of affairs in the mass media, according to both mainsteam and advocacy press journalists.

James Weinstein, editor of the weekly advocacy press *In These Times,* compared the content of *Harper's* and the *Atlantic Monthly*—monthly magazines of opinion, literature, and culture—with his own publication: "You get stories on what's happening to the national parks—not that that's not important, but it's not what's affecting our readers." In the 12-year period studied here, *Atlantic Monthly* had two articles on occupational health; *Harper's*, none.

Richard Severo, an investigative reporter for the *New York Times,* was more critical of the reasons for sparse coverage of occupational health in the mainstream press.

> These kinds of stories are irksome to industry. My national editor liked the story (on genetic screening) a lot, but didn't submit it for any awards. The response was muted. . . . Most papers are capitalist institutions and have only limited interest in this subject.

Most advocacy press reporters agreed with Severo, saying that time and economic interests precluded coverage of the topic by the daily press. In the words of *The Progressive* editor, Robert Buell, "Occupational health is a dangerous issue—especially exploring what little has been done and why. It's a pandora's box."

Yet the advocacy press has not devoted a great deal of space to occupational health either. Editors were apologetic when asked about their coverage; several pointed to their lack of resources and staff, a perennial problem for most small press publications. Even so, their coverage differs from that of the mainstream in the choice of events and style of coverage.

CONCEPTUALIZATIONS: CONFLICTS OR CONSENSUS

Advocacy press reporters conceptualize occupational health in the broad context of capitalism and economic power, focusing on exploitation, coercion, and manipulation of workers by both big business and government. Jumpers are desperate men and women exploited by ruthless nuclear industry executives; pesticide workers are exposed to dangerous substances due to negligence. In effect, the advocacy press conveys a conflict model of social reality.

Mainstream press reporters, on the other hand, convey a consensus view of the social system when they write about occupational health. Government and industry work together to develop and follow safety standards to benefit nuclear workers; when an occupational illness is discovered, government and industry respond quickly to remove its cause. Consistent with this consensus model is the tendency to blame hazards on the irresponsibility of a few bad companies, ignorance, or lack of prudence, rather than on deliberate disregard of health and safety or the structure of industry-labor relations.[3] Mark Misercola, former labor reporter for the defunct *Courier Express,* blamed a few backward companies for much of the occupational illness problem:

> There are a lot of bad companies . . . they should know better by now. . . . I don't think there's much of an excuse for it now. (Older failing industries) who don't look out for their workers are the major culprits.

Robert Cunningham, of the *Bergen Record* in Hackensack, New Jersey, chalked up problems to ignorance:

> People did not know 20 years ago—although there is some evidence that there was more knowledge than we thought—perceiving something happening 20 years afterwards is hard. It's a difficult thing to grasp. Imagine a press conference a few years ago where somebody got up and said workers are going to die 20 years from now. "Yeah, sure buddy."

A colleague at the mainstream newsweekly also doubted outright industry negligence: "I've sometimes wondered if people sit down and calculate the cost of this versus the cost of that. I think it's expedience or just not very much common sense."

Suggested causes of and solutions to occupational hazards in mainstream and advocacy press articles also reflect the conflict/consensus dichotomy. Articles from both presses offer scenarios ranging from the cosmic—basic American or

TABLE 3.2
Thematic Analysis of Suggested Causes of
Occupational Hazards in Mainstream and Advocacy Press

Causes	Press	
	Mainstream	Advocacy
Structural: total	15　(7.0%)*	28　(32%)*
U. S. Socioeconomic values		10
Profits/productivity link	10	9
Government/industry ties, industry dominance	1	7
Industry regulatory lobbying	3	
Congressional resistance and lack of policy making	1	2
Bureaucratic/Technical: total	56　(28.3%)*	15　(17.4%)*
"Progress"	12	7
Red-tape: Poor enforcement, lack of funding, staff	22	6
Difficult to make diagnosis	16	2
Genetic weakness	1	
Workers' lifestyles	4	
Work inherently risky	1	
Number of articles coded	213	86

NOTE: The totals listed here are summary figures of all statements and news source comments referring to the causes of health hazards found in the 299 articles I coded. The specific category headings, or "themes," are generalizations of those statements.
*A chi-square test of these four percentages shows that the differences between the two presses' suggested causes is statistically significant. Chi-square = 22.06; $p < .005$; d.f. = 1.

industrial values—to the mundane—lack of staff and funding for OSHA. However, the relative emphasis given to these scenarios differs. Table 3.2 shows the differences between mainstream and advocacy press in their characterization of the causes of occupational hazards.

The technical/bureaucratic orientation of the daily and weekly mainstream press is reflected in articles focusing on foul-ups at OSHA and on scientific and technical problems, such as the introduction of new, more toxic chemicals.

For example, *U.S. News and World Report* reported on "frivolous safety rules" and on the lack of safety standards for government workers (who are not covered by OSHA). An

April 1975 article entitled "A Double Standard for Safety Rules?" pointed out the disparity in safety standards for public and private sector employees, implying that the government was acting tough on private industry but shirking its responsibility to protect its own workers. A June 1980 piece, "If Government Had to Dance to OSHA's Tune," cast an embarrassing light on the federal government by revealing inadequate safety practices in government offices.

The advocacy press focused less on government red tape than on the structural links between government and industry that lead to occupational hazards. For example, in articles on government-controlled uranium mines, *In These Times* argues that the practice of industry subcontracting from the federal government conveniently protected corporations from OSHA inspections, to the detriment of workers. The advocacy press also emphasized the "unbridled corporate power" wielded over workers in one-mill towns. *Mother Jones's* coverage of the California Department of Agriculture and the pesticide DBCP excoriated the abuses arising from the political and economic ties between government and industry. The advocacy press does not assume that corporations are socially responsible, and then attempt to expose instances of flawed responsibility. Instead, it prefers to show the "unacceptable face of capitalism."[4]

The suggested solutions to occupational hazards summarized in Table 3.3 also indicate differing journalistic perspectives of the social order. Although an approximately equal proportion of suggested solutions in both presses center around government action (6.6% to 5.8%), there are noticeable differences in the proposals for other solutions.

The advocacy press is inclined to suggest workplace action, such as strikes, the establishment of union health and safety committees, and active citizen/worker coalitions, to eliminate occupational hazards. Of the solutions proposed by the advocacy press, 19% (16 of 86) suggest workplace action, compared to 9% (17 of 213) in the mainstream publications. In the advo-

TABLE 3.3
Thematic Analysis of Suggested Solutions to
Occupational Health Problems in Mainstream and Advocacy Press

	Press			
Solutions	Mainstream		Advocacy	
Governmental response: total	14	(6.6%)	5	(5.8%)
Strengthen and enforce law	7		2	
New legislation, Congressional hearings	3		1	
Criminal prosecution			1	
Allocate more resources			1	
Litigation	2			
Wage tax to finance research	1			
Better compensation system	1			
Workplace action: total	17	(9%)	16	(19%)
Technical:				
Engineering controls	4			
Better work practices, training, medical facilities, and equipment	5		2	
Labor:				
Strike			4	
Active union local or safety comte.	7		9	
Worker/citizen involvement in research			1	
Workers take better care of themselves	1			
Societal change: total	2	(.9%)	12	(13.9%)
Labor party formation			1	
Informed citizenry/"public hysteria"	2		3	
Make corporate accountability to the public a legitimate concept			8	
Number of articles coded	213		86	

NOTE: The totals listed here are summary figures of all statements and news source comments referring to the solutions to health hazards found in the 299 articles I coded. The specific category headings, or "themes," are generalizations of those statements.

cacy press activism is regarded positively as a source of social change. Articles emphasize the need for strong, militant union action and worker participation to combat the interests of the corporate elite.

In contrast, the mainstream press focuses on technical solutions, including engineering controls, better equipment, medical facilities, and training—all means of "fine tuning" an otherwise reasonably well-functioning system. As the mainstream press located the source of occupational hazards in inefficient bureaucracy and inadequate scientific knowledge, it is not surprising to find that suggested solutions emphasize improved government and more rationalized technical procedures.[5] The coverage of the Connecticut Yankee nuclear power plan shutdown reflected these differences. The *Times* stories focused on the necessity for small-scale bureaucratic revisions of procedure; the advocacy press coverage stressed labor issues, especially the usefulness of health and safety strikes at nuclear facilities.

SOURCES

Mainstream and advocacy press articles about occupational health also differ in their use of news sources. The advocacy press gives substantially more coverage to labor sources, whereas mainstream press reporters mainly call upon government sources to explain the background of regulatory decisions, standards, and other technically based policy decisions (see Tables 3.4 and 3.5). In many of the *New York Times* articles about the nuclear industry no workers—even those affected by the subject of the piece—are quoted. *The Progressive* and *In These Times* extensively quoted uranium miners, jumpers, and pesticide workers about shop floor practices.

There are a number of reasons for this differential use of sources. First, workers may be reluctant to talk on the record to inquisitive reporters. Rachel Scott, author of *Muscle and Blood*, a study of workers in dangerous jobs, told a conference of journalists and bureaucrats of her experience in writing about the topic:

> Now this may be unusual, this may be just my experience, but very often the worker has the most to lose by talking to you . . . they could

TABLE 3.4

Comparison of Number of Sources, Government and Labor,
in Mainstream and Advocacy Press

	Number of Actors				
Press	Government		Labor		
Advocacy	66	(22)	162	(48)	228
Mainstream	252	(37)	212	(31)	464
	318		374		692

NOTE: Numbers in parentheses are percentages. They do not total 100% because table does not include other news source categories. Chi-square = 30.4; p. < .001; d.f. = 1. With Yate's correction for small sample size.

TABLE 3.5

Comparison of Space, Government and Labor Sources,
in Mainstream of Advocacy Press

	Amount of Space in Inches				
Press	Government		Labor		
Advocacy	92.5	(17.2)	444.5	(82.5)	537
Mainstream	369.0	(56.5)	284.0	(43.5)	653
	461.5		728.5		1190

NOTE: Chi-square = 191.7; p < .001; d.f. = 1. With Yates's correction for small sample size.

lose their job . . . they could be harassed in other ways . . . so workers very often speak in spite of the fact that they are taking a very big risk.[6]

Many workers aren't willing to take the risk and, hence, are problematic as sources. Moreover, they are not easily contacted. Scott recounts hours of standing outside plant gates, taking down people's names and phone numbers. At the same conference, Michael Flannery of the *Chicago Sun Times* tells of spending many months cultivating sources, visiting plants and union halls.

Many mainstream reporters do not visit plants or follow up on workers' tips because the workers lack official status or because they are not assumed to be competent reporters of factory life. Sociologists Mortenson and Svendson noted this:

"Just call the chairman" was a set routine in many of the local papers. A worker who had worked for 39 years at an iron foundry was not judged by one editor to be a competent person as a source about his destroyed lungs. The journalist had to counterbalance the evidence through an interview with the director who denied any relationship between mineral dust particles and silicosis. In this instance, the journalist was sufficiently involved to engage a third source, a physician, who agreed with the worker. This counterbalancing ritual is not started when it is an authoritative source who pronounces.[7]

Similarly, *Bergen Record* reporter Robert Kravitz, when asked what would happen if a worker called with a tip on dangerous work practices, stated, "If it's just one worker calling it's almost impossible to follow up." And labor reporter Mark Misercola said he'd have to wait for something official: "I'd tell my boss (about the tip) and nine times out of ten, he'd say, well, if something official hasn't been filed, we can't do anything. That was the typical response." Misercola's managing director, Joel Kramer, concurred with Misercola's view:

There are two basic ways to find out about a story . . . the first is for some insider in the company to call, some insider who was not able to get action through the government or the company. It didn't happen when I was at the *Courier*. The only stories we did were the ones raised by government agencies or labor groups.

Workers, unlike plant managers, owners, and politicians, work behind closed factory gates with little discretion to talk to reporters during the working day, and they seldom share the same outlook as reporters. As *Wall Street Journal* reporter Karen Rothmeyer observed:

The biggest problem for a daily reporter (is that) . . . middle-class journalists who are used to dealing with middle-class officials won't get off their asses to make the difficult effort to find people on the other side. You've got to get out and talk with elderly, sick, working-class Southerners who may not even be sure that it's important to talk to the

press. Too many reporters wind up being Establishment stooges, not
because they're uncaring people but because they're middle class and
don't want to struggle with speaking another language with different
people.[8]

NEWSPEGS

A comparison of newspegs in three weeklies—*Newsweek,
U.S. News,* and *In These Times*—also indicates differing
emphases. A newspeg is the event, activity, or controversy that
provides the angle for a news account. *U.S. News* has the
largest percentage of articles with a newspeg about legislative,
executive, or judicial action, or the release of a scientific report
(78%). While *ITT* and *Newsweek* had similar percentages of
this newspeg (36% and 42%, respectively), *ITT* was the only
one of the three publications to use union activities as newspegs
(16%).

In interviews, some reporters alluded to this lack of coverage
of workplace organizing for health and safety improvements.
A newsweekly reporter confessed that her publication had
skimped on covering issues of workplace democracy. Mark
Misercola of the *Courier Express* complained that his newspaper vacillated in its commitment to a regular labor beat;
when he left the paper, the labor beat died with him. His
managing editor, Joel Kramer, stated the following:

> We covered it whenever we thought it was appropriate. I can't
> remember a story worth doing about occupational health while I've
> been here [about 2 years]. The economic story was the big story in
> Buffalo. Doing stories on conditions in the steel plants would be like
> kicking a dying animal.

Advocacy reporters believed that for most journalists, labor
coverage was "low on the totem pole," a brief "stepping stone"
toward more glamorous beats like politics. Robert Howard,

who worked for *In These Times* and now works for the labor-
oriented monthly *Working Papers,* stated: "To do this stuff
well requires a kind of expertise that's very hard to define—to
capture what really goes on in the workplace." He doubted
most mainstream reporters had that expertise; if they did, they
were constrained by editors who were not interested in labor
coverage. Some mainstream publications seemed to define
labor coverage as standing outside the plant gate or attending a
press conference to hear what a union official had to say; few
reported having set foot inside a plant to cover a story or do a
feature.

ANALYSIS:
NEWS AS IDEOLOGY

Ideology is both a political and cultural concept. Ideologies,
according to anthropologist Clifford Geertz, do more than
simply direct political movement; they also provide "schematic
images of the social order," offering both cognitive systems of
thought and expressive symbols as a means of comprehending
the universe.[9] The analysis of news accounts of occupational
health suggests that both the mainstream and advocacy presses
convey a relatively consistent ideology in the sense intended by
Geertz. Their linguistic cues, their use of news sources, their
recurrent themes convey strikingly different conceptualiza-
tions of the issue to the public.

The mainstream press conveys a consensus view of society:
Workplace hazards result from the practices of a few negligent
companies; the government has passed reasonably adequate,
generally beneficial laws and will pass stricter ones in the future
as more data come in; the effectiveness of these measures may
be mitigated by bureaucratic inefficiency or scientific uncertainty; even so, industry—prompted by sometimes overzealous
regulators—will clean up the workplace, protect workers, and

continually improve work practices; government power is primary, and elected officials promulgate policy and formulate technical solutions in a rational way to the overall benefit of everyone.

The advocacy press coverage of these same issues tends toward a conflict view. This view stresses that workplace hazards are an integral part of corporate practice and policy; that the government functions primarily for the benefit of corporate profitability, not the public good; that the interests of workers and business always are opposed to each other; and that coercion and threat are necessary to minimize conflict over occupational health and safety.

To suggest that one of these perspectives is "biased" or "subjective" and the other "neutral" and "objective" is to misunderstand the nature of news accounts. Although articles in the mainstream press are couched in the language customarily characterized as neutral, in fact the coverage of events in both presses follows from ideologically guided choices of what to emphasize and in what context.

In asserting that news is ideological I am considering both its character as a text and the means by which it is produced. Ideology as I define it here is systematic, selective perception. News accounts are texts that convey meaning—but in order to do so, the journalists who construct them must make choices. News stories are ideological because they cannot be about everything—they inevitably involve selection, whether it is the choice to cover an occupational health strike or an environmental disaster, to quote officials or workers, to blame one industry or the capitalist system.

As sociologist Paul Weaver points out, every news story has a politics: Through the choice of language, the news angle, the use of sources, even the sentence structure itself, news propagates opinion as well as information. Weaver calls this selective character of a news story its "social competence": "The kinds of questions it invites a reader to pursue and enables him to answer . . . or the kinds of questions it discourages and does not equip a reader to answer or think about."[10]

Others make similar observations about the selective character of news. Sociologist Gaye Tuchman observes that the world is an endless chaos of occurrences, any of which is a potential news story. "News organizations must sort out these claims of occurrences . . . [they] must reduce all phenomena to constructed classifications. . . . i.e., news organizations must select real world occurrences in order to facilitate carrying out the daily demands of news work."[11] There is, according to Mark Fishman, no determinant reality out there that reporters simply translate to an awaiting public; rather, journalists create the news by calling upon the standard operating procedures of their craft.[12]

Beyond the question of selectivity, news also is ideological because of certain professional practices that involve implicit "frames" of society and politics. Harvey Molotch points out that "the most proximate force shaping the nose for news is the unrelenting demand that reporters provide large quantities of copy each day."[13] This technical constraint has its own ideological implications. The daily need for copy spurs journalists in the daily press to find "dependable" sources of copy—the established bureaucrats, who provide material through press conferences, press releases, and professional media liaisons. Their pronouncements have legitimacy, and it is simply assumed that they also are competent to know.

Molotch sums it up:

> "[R]eporters become locked in established bureaucracies because only these institutions have both prima facie legitimacy and are dependable sources of column inches of copy."[14]

Advocacy press journalists do not work under the same time pressure—they work on a weekly or monthly schedule. Partly for this reason, they are less dependent on immediately available official sources of news.

Professional practices also import ideology through the beat system, set up originally to facilitate reliable news gathering for expanding newspaper space. As practiced nowadays, the beat system shapes ideological assumptions implying news judgments about who commands legitimate power and knowledge. The beat is more than a road map for the reporter's activities: "It implicitly contains an ideology that continually informs the reporter what the beat is all about . . . this includes such things as who on the beat is entitled to know what, who is an interested party, what occurrences fall outside the spectrum of potentially newsworthy events."[15]

For its coverage of occupational health, the mainstream press grants legitimacy to elected officials and other political and economic elites. Those who hold legitimate positions of power have more access to the media than those who do not. Lower-class groups, workers, the poor, dissidents, and radicals are simply assumed to be illegitimate and unnewsworthy sources. These assumptions of legitimacy distinguish mainstream and advocacy press reporting of specific topics like DBCP and jumpers. It is interesting to note here Victor Navasky's remarks on the way his advocacy press magazine, *The Nation*, uses its staff: He employs the "kamikaze method" of reporting; reporters spend time on a beat for only one story, lest they internalize their news sources' values and perceptions. Navasky criticizes mainstream press journalists for spending too much time in Washington, shoulder to shoulder with political elites; *The Nation*, he argues, prefers to avoid national political cliques in favor of bottom-up coverage of workers' and citizens' views.[16]

Finally, news is ideological as the result of professional socialization. A publication's editorial policy is internalized in reporters' minds: The socialization of newcomers, the use of formal authority and sanctions, and the reporters' desire for smooth career advancement reinforce editorial pressures.[17]

Self-selection also comes into play: Most advocacy press journalists work where they do because their notions of their
professional role differ from those of mainstream journalists.
They wish to educate and incite, rather than inform and enter-
tain. The result is to turn reporters into "hypothesis testers,"
searching out confirmation for their preconceptions about the
meaning of news events.[18]

Journalists quickly learn what their publications expect of
them. They find out that occupational health stories are "irk-
some to industry"; that they are taken off beats or reined in if
they are too zealous in pursuing corporate wrongdoing; that it
is easier and more professionally rewarding to cover the routine sources of news. They avoid challenging their sources,
because to do so would cut off further interaction, and because
they commonly share the same personal and professional outlooks. However, in advocacy press publications, journalists
learn that muckraking and criticism of government and industry are valued. Thus, publications like *The Progressive, In
These Times*, and *Mother Jones* are forums in which news and
views ignored in the mainstream press can get a hearing.

These conflicting orientations of mainstream and advocacy
press accounts do not have equal sway in the public mind,
because the presses do not enjoy equal status in the information environment. The mass media claim overwhelming economic and structural dominance. In 1970, for example, the top
five newspaper firms accounted for 71% of circulation; the top
five broadcast, cinema, paperback book, and record companies accounted for, on the average, 69% of circulation in their
sectors.[19] Despite the recent surge in the new technologies, such
as satellites and cable TV, that have increased the number of
media outlets, there has been little substantive change in the
relationship of advocacy and "alternative" voices to the mass
media.

The drive toward stable profitability in the 1970s has meant
further concentration, so that media sectors increasingly are

dominated by a few large companies. As Murdock and Golding point out, "conglomeration enables the [corporations] to significantly extend their potential control over the 'production and distribution of the ideas of their age.' "[20]

The advocacy press has the potential to change public attitudes by contradicting predominant views, but it is at a distinct disadvantage in doing so. In an environment in which communications companies are enmeshed with other corporate and financial interests, economically marginal advocacy publications—the journals of opinion, the left-wing political weeklies and monthlies, the small press publishers—are bucking strong headwind in their struggle to disseminate alternative views. The mainstream media have more outlets, more frequent publications, more circulation, and more stable sources of financing, and, hence, substantially greater legitimacy to define social reality. They are powerful institutions not simply because they command impressive outlays of capital, nor because their efforts might garner votes or sell products; they are powerful because the opportunity to "selectively maintain relatively stable structures of images and associations" is the power to define the policy agenda.[21]

Occupational health is only one of the many problems of technological risk that require understanding a bewildering and often disputed array of technical information in the context of complex political relationships. Although both presses are highly selective in their approaches to the problem, the advocacy press cultivates a crucial political resource for dealing with risks: a critically informed citizenry more concerned with the health and welfare of workers than the health and welfare of industry. Such concern, whether spurred by press coverage or nurtured by sharp political struggle, is the necessary first step to ending the contradiction between work and health.

NOTES

1. The citations to individual news accounts are included in the body of the text. The term "advocacy press" is meant to encompass a number of terms that have been used at one time or another to refer to avowedly opinionated journalism, including "muckraking," "political," "new," or "alternative" journalism. For a more detailed examination of the history of mainstream and advocacy press journalism and the notion of objectivity, see Chris Anne Raymond, "Uncovering Ideology: Occupational Health in the Mainstream and Advocacy Press, 1970-82" (Ph.D. diss., Cornell University, 1983).

2. See, for example, Bob Hall, "The Brown-Lung Controversy," *Columbia Journalism Review*, March 1978, pp. 27-35; Ray Marshall, *Lost in the Workplace: Is There an Occupational Health Epidemic?* (Washington, DC: Department of Labor, 1979); Betty Medsger, "Asbestos: The California Story," *Columbia Journalism Review*, July 1977, pp. 23-27.

3. For a discussion of mainstream reporters' beliefs about government and business, see Herbert Gans, *Deciding What's News* (New York: Pantheon, 1979).

4. John Westergaard, "Power, Class and the Media," in *Mass Communication and Society*, eds. James Curran et al. (Beverly Hills, CA: Sage, 1977), pp. 95-115.

5. The difference in observed frequencies of "technical" and "labor" solutions in the two press articles is statistically significant. Chi-square = 6.04; $p < .01$; d.f. = 1.

6. Marshall, *Lost in the Workplace*.

7. Frank Mortenson and Erik Nordahl Svendsen, "Creativity and Control: The Journalist Betwixt His Readers and Editors," *Critical Sociology* 7 (1980): 182.

8. Bob Hall, "The Brown-Lung Controversy," p. 35.

9. Clifford Geertz, "Ideology as a Cultural System," in *Ideology and Discontent*, ed. David Apter (New York: Free Press, 1964), pp. 46-76.

10. Paul Weaver, "The Politics of a News Story," in *The Mass Media and Modern Democracy*, ed. Harry M. Clor (Chicago: Rand McNally, 1974), pp. 85-111.

11. Gaye Tuchman, "The Exception Proves the Rule: The Study of Routine News Practices," in *Strategies for Communications Research*, eds. Paul M. Hirsch et al. (Beverly Hills, CA: Sage, 1977), pp. 43-61.

12. See Mark Fishman, *Manufacturing the News* (Austin: University of Texas Press, 1980).

13. See Harvey Molotch, "Media and Movements," in *The Dynamics of Social Movements*, eds. Mayer N. Zald and John D. McCarthy (Boston: Little, Brown, 1979), pp. 71-90.

14. Ibid., p. 76.

15. Fishman, *Manufacturing the News*, p. 43.

16. Victor Navasky, "Some Marks of Distinction in The Nation's Journalism," *Center Magazine*, May 1981, pp. 5-14.

17. Lee Sigelman, "Reporting the News: An Organizational Analysis," *American Journal of Sociology* 79 (1973): 132-151; Warren Breed, "Social Control in the Newsroom: A Functional Analysis," *Social Forces* 83 (1955): 326-335.

18. Sigelman, "Reporting the News."

19. Graham Murdock and Peter Golding, "Capitalism, Communication, and Class Relations," in *Mass Communication and Society,* ed. James Curran (Beverly Hills, CA: Sage, 1979), pp. 12-43.

20. Ibid., p. 28.

21. George Gerbner, "Communication and Social Environment," *Scientific American* 227 (1972): 152-160.

4

ETHICAL CONFLICTS IN OCCUPATIONAL MEDICINE

Dorothy Nelkin

In his opening remarks at a conference on the ethical issues of occupational medicine, Norbert J. Roberts, former medical director of Exxon Corporation, stated, "Those of us who practice occupational medicine have understood ourselves to be bound by the general principles of ethical conduct for physicians."[1] Quite a different view comes from labor. Sheldon Samuels, health and safety director of the AFL-CIO put it bluntly: "With a few brilliant exceptions, company doctors reflect the crud of the medical profession."[2]

The gap between the self-image of occupational physicians and the perceptions of their patients is profound. While company doctors are guided by professional codes of ethics that stress their commitment to patients, their professional image is tarnished by the context in which they work. Their association with a company committed to profitable production leaves them highly suspect.

The conflict and distrust that pervade the ethics of corporate medicine must be understood in terms that are independent of the profession's own ideology, an ideology that stresses the ethical norms and scientific knowledge that guide professional medical practice. A more analytic approach would rather

Author's Note: *Valuable criticism was provided by Michael Brown, Arthur Caplan, Stephen Hilgartner, and Diana Chapman Walsh.*

emphasize the importance of the institutional and cultural context in shaping professional behavior.[3] That is, the practice of corporate medicine necessarily reflects not only the intentions and ideology of the profession, but also the practical constraints and cultural biases of its institutional environment.

After examining the conflicting images of occupational medicine, I will review the economic, social, and cultural realities of medical practice in a corporate setting and suggest their effect on the ability of company doctors to implement the intentions set forth in the ethical guidelines of their profession.

TWO IMAGES OF A CONTROVERSIAL PROFESSION

The corporate physician's self-image is codified in the ethical guidelines of the American Occupational Medical Association. This code of ethical conduct, adopted in July 1976, specifies:

> Physicians should accord highest priority to the health and safety of the individual in the workplace; practice on a scientific basis with objectivity and integrity; make or endorse only statements which reflect their observations or honest opinion; . . . avoid allowing their medical judgment to be influenced by any conflict of interest.[4]

The guidelines also specify ethical conduct with respect to the handling of information; the physician should "treat as confidential whatever is learned about individuals served, releasing information only when required by law or by overriding public health considerations . . . and recognize that employers are entitled to counsel about the medical fitness of individuals in relation to work, but are not entitled to diagnoses or details." Physicians must also "communicate information about health hazards in timely and effective fashion to individuals or groups potentially affected; . . . [and] communicate understandably to those they serve any significant observations about their health."

These codes are reinforced by legal precedents that have established that confidentiality must be maintained unless the patient gives fully informed consent to the disclosure, that physicians must provide accurate information to patients, and that they cannot misrepresent a patient's condition to prevent compensation. Failure to adequately inform patients has been construed as negligence by the courts. However, in other decisions the courts have found that the obligation to inform rests not with the physician, but with the employer.[5]

Company doctors are confronted with frequent criticisms, both from their patients and from other physicians. They clearly are aware of the ambiguities inherent in their role. In response to accusations of ethical misconduct and bias due to their divided loyalties, they strongly defend their integrity, their scientific objectivity, and, above all, their primary allegiance to the patient. Irving Tabershaw, M.D., a leading spokesman for the profession, writes that the physician is a professional. "He works for no other purpose than the benefit of his patients. In occupational medicine that is the worker . . . the physician is *not* an agent of industry."[6] Tabershaw and other physicians emphasize that they are operating according to the same norms that guide all physicians and that the poor reputation of the profession is but an obsolete vestige of the old days of one-company mining towns. Although they admit there may be poor practitioners, they insist that these are simply the few aberrant individuals that exist in every profession. Parry Norling, director of health and safety at DuPont, expressed the prevailing view: "In any field the excellent results of the 99% who are responsible are quickly forgotten when the remaining 1% make mistakes, are thoughtless, or are just plain irresponsible."[7]

Corporate physicians reconcile the ambiguities in their role on the basis of two related beliefs: a faith in the existence of a social consensus in which shared values are the fundamental characteristic of a society and the basis of social organization, and a belief that the scientific objectivity of professional practice overrides all conflicts of interest, placing doctors outside of partisan disputes.

Most company doctors share with corporate managers a set of beliefs about how American society works. They believe that the economic system is reasonable, efficient, and fundamentally nonexploitative, that protecting workers' health is a common goal, a goal that is shared by management and labor alike. There is, they are convinced, a fundamental confluence of interest between management and labor and between the goals of a profitable enterprise and the interests of society as a whole.[8] For example, a widely published advertisement by the Chemical Manufacturers' Association portrays a company physician, a kindly middle-aged woman who says, "Our company's greatest asset is our employees. Their health and safety are our number one priority."

Convinced that workers and management have a common interest in the health and safety of the workplace, company doctors often refer to the "seeming" or "apparent" conflict, arguing that the healthy worker is more productive for industry and that therefore companies have a profit incentive in protecting worker health. Robert R. Hilker, M.D., corporate medical director of Illinois Bell Telephone Company, asserts that "we aren't in an adversary position at all. Our job is to do the best we can for patients within the business setting. We are simply another part of the health care system."[9] Bertrand Dinman, M.D., a physician for the Aluminum Company of America, holds the view that the corporation as well as the worker is a patient. He argues that "in preventing harm to employees, the physician fulfills his responsibility to the corporate patient as well."[10] Bruce W. Karrh, M.D., Corporate Medical Director and Vice President of DuPont, refers to his company's "traditional concern" for employee health—a concern that is reflected in five principles that guide health policy: "knowledge, commitment, responsibility, compliance, and communications."[11] These principles, based on "good, sound business practice," are entirely in accord with the ethical responsibilities of the physician. There is, in other words, no conflict between the goals of a profitable and productive enterprise and the health of its workers.

Company doctors also reconcile their dual loyalties through continued reference to the scientific roots of their profession. Company doctors insist that both their medical judgments concerning their patients and their professional advice to management are based on solid, objective evidence "on correct science with respect to medical evidence."[12] They emphasize their "neutrality" and their "professionalism." They adhere to what one sociologist has called "the dogma of immaculate perception,"[13] that professional practice mainly involves straightforward observation and data collection that is uninfluenced by the social context.

A Canadian study of the conflicting pressures facing company doctors found that corporate medical practices tended to be biased toward management priorities. However, the doctors interviewed saw themselves as objective and neutral, outside of partisan disputes. Their professional ideology, based on assumptions about the scientific nature of medicine, inhibited recognition of the conflicts of interest that they confronted every day.[14]

Faith in the scientific objectivity of professional practice allows company doctors to separate their administrative and medical roles and to believe that their advisory and adjudicatory responsibilities, even in compensation cases, will not influence their medical (i.e., objective) judgment concerning the complaints of workers/patients. Their belief in the neutrality of expertise also serves to justify and encourage paternalistic practices with respect to information. It becomes reasonable in this context to withhold information from workers in order to avoid misinterpretation of complex technical materials or to prevent undue alarm. It becomes justifiable to impose job restrictions—even without employee consent—as in the best interests of both workers and the firm.

The picture that emerges from interviews with workers and statements by health activists in the labor movement totally contradicts the company doctor's view. In contrast to the consensus model underlying physicians' beliefs, many workers assume there is a basic conflict between social groups, and that social order merely reflects the ability of powerful groups to dominate others and manipulate their consent. In their view, experts (in this case, company doctors) are complicit in this relationship. They therefore see them as "agents" or "pawns" of management.[15] A granulator at a large pharmaceutical plant provides a typical and bleak point of view:

> From what I understand, our company doctor was an engineer that the company put through medical school. He's their pawn, and he does what they say. He'll never back an employee. We're required to take a physical every two years. They say it's for our benefit.

> We don't want no physicals, and we don't want anything from them. If they want us to take physicals, we want to be able to go to our own physician and have them pay the cost. We want to have the medical people here for emergency treatment, but for nothing else.

Similarly, a chemical operator feels the company doctor is simply an agent of the firm:

> I went to the company doctor and he's queerer than a three-dollar bill. As far as I'm concerned, he's doing me no good at all. All he's worrying about is protecting the company. They give exams to protect themselves. It's all whitewash.

Workers tend to distinguish the company doctor from their private physician. Some deliberately call their company doctor "Mister," in order not to denigrate the profession as a whole. A filter cleaner in a pharmaceutical plant goes to the company doctor only with reluctance:

> The only time I go there is if I have an accident, or they call me for a physical. They're hatchet men. They're not there for the benefit of the employees, they're there to keep you quiet and to put on a show for

OSHA or the government or whoever. It's a farce. I trust my own doctor; I believe what he says to me, and I believe that he's working in the best interests of my health. The company doctor isn't doing that. In most cases he's a guy who has gone to industry because the pressures of private practice are too great. If you work for management you just do what they say, get paid, and go home.

Having little faith in the confidentiality of records, workers suspect that their medical records will be used against them. Thus, some avoid contact with the medical department if they can. A welder in a chemical plant claims that he avoids the doctor even when he is sick:

One fella had blips on his lungs and he has emphysema. He told me because I work with him every day, but he wants to keep it a secret from the company because he's afraid that the company will use it against him.

A worker in a manufacturing plant describes how medical records can restrict employees:

I wanted to do a job that was on the line, but the foreman told me I couldn't: "It says in your file that you can't work with that black wax spray and Triad [trichloroethylene]." I immediately went to the nurse's office. She says, "Don't you remember the time you came in to the doctor and he took you off the Triad?" "Yeah, he took me off, for a period of six weeks. He didn't say it was going to be indefinite." They took the restriction off. You better find out what they're writing in your medical record, because I was restricted and didn't even know it.

Suspecting that medical records will harm her, a laboratory technician in a pharmaceutical plant refuses to use the company medical services:

I won't take my dog to the company doctor. He's all company. I try not to go because that's on your record from the day you're there to the day you leave the place; everything bad you do stays with you.

Many workers, however, do use corporate medical facilities. In some cases, corporate regulations require employees to go to company doctors for routine medical exams and to file complaints. Workers also use company doctors because it saves them money, or because they have no private physician. Those who choose to go to their own doctor often find that physicians in private practice are unfamiliar with problems of occupational health and see too few patients to draw meaningful diagnostic conclusions about work-induced complaints. A fire fighter exposed to PCBs sent his blood tests to his doctor: "He told me they didn't do him any good—he didn't know how to read them." Although they fear that medical records can be used against them to screen them out of a job, workers also know that these records will be necessary if they ever make a compensation claim, for they may provide evidence of symptoms that later show up as an occupationally-related disease.

Workers also are concerned about the quality of care provided by company doctors. They feel their complaints are ignored or trivialized. Workers often suggest that company doctors trivialize the nature and extent of their problems in order to get them back to work: "No matter what's wrong with you, you go back to work." "They make people go back to work before they should." An air conditioning repairman complained of dizziness:

> They just said, "Well, have you had a cold lately? Did you go out last night and get drunk?" Then they lost the lab reports on a couple of men who went down for blood tests. The guys were very upset. They said, "To hell with it" and went to their family doctors.

They also fear that medical judgments reflect the need to absolve the company from responsibility. A chemical operator went to the company doctor complaining of massive headaches:

> He told me I had hardening of the arteries and gave me a prescription. I didn't know what they were, but I took them and still got the headaches. I was out of work for eight or nine days. Nothing seemed to be getting any better, so finally I said screw this, I'm going to a neurologist. I explained the headaches and showed him the pills that the other doctor gave me. They were cortisone. He threw them in the garbage and said that I shouldn't be getting those at all, that I was too young for arteriosclerosis. I explained to him about being hit with phosgene during an accident at the plant. He thought there was a possibility that was the cause, but there was no way to prove it.

Finally, workers also mistrust the information given to them by corporate medical departments. They want access to their own records and also data on exposure levels and general health conditions in their plant so as to better understand their own health problems, to take appropriate precautions, or to document their claims for compensation. A federal rule now requires disclosure of information on request. Moreover, the ethics of medical practice require "timely and effective" communication about both health hazards in the workplace and individual exposures. Yet a computer assembler at a manufacturing plant who asked the company doctor for access to his records, described the response:

> The doctor, he was really cold. I went in and he kind of half hid the records. The main thing that I wanted to see was my exposure because I work with all these chemicals, but they didn't have that. He asked me why I wanted that, and I told him flat out, "Listen, if I come down with something in the future, I want it on the record that I worked with these chemicals." He proceeded to tell me there was nothing wrong with the chemicals at this plant, that in his 35 years of being a company doctor he had never seen an occupational-related disease. I knew better. The man was just flat-out lying to me. What choice do you have when you have to go to people like that?

He continued on about a friend who went to the doctor because of a rash on her arm:

The doctor told her she was holding her screwdriver wrong. I mean, that was bullshit. It was a chemical problem, because she was working with methyl chloroform, so that authority figure, that company doctor, is telling people this and they're figuring, "Well, he's a doctor, he should know."

Few workers have any sense that company doctors are part of a profession with a formal set of ethical principles that guide their practice. Rather, they perceive corporate medicine as a means to protect the firm against lawsuits and compensation claims, to reduce insurance premiums, to minimize sick leaves, or to deny the need for costly investment in health and safety equipment. In 1982, a union magazine, *The Chemical Worker*, summarized labor's image of corporate medicine:

The company doctor cares about the financial health of the company, not your physical health: workers are given exams for very specific reasons: 1) to ensure productivity by screening out workers unable to perform jobs they are assigned to, 2) to try to block later compensation claims or to minimize the size of the award, 3) because they are forced to by certain OSHA standards, 4) to harass and discriminate against workers the company wants to get rid of.[16]

Suspicion and mistrust of corporate medical professionals is endemic among workers, who regard company doctors as adversaries in a social context characterized by conflicting values and goals.

THE CONTEXT OF CORPORATE MEDICINE

The ethics of a profession, as embodied in codes, guidelines, and public declarations, are but statements of intention. They may have little to do with the actual content of professional work. According to sociologist Eliot Freidson, in his book on the profession of medicine, the content and therefore the ethics of professional work must be considered in terms of the social and economic organization of the work setting. The economic and career stakes of practitioners and the administrative needs of their institutions all influence the physicians' interpretations of illness and judgments about its management. "So far as the terms of work go," says Freidson, "professions differ from trade unions only in their sanctimoniousness."[17]

We also must consider company doctors in terms of what anthropologist Mary Douglas calls the "cultural bias" or world view characteristic of their institution. She argues that people's perceptions of and attitudes toward both risk and health are strongly colored by their institutional culture.[18] Thus, understanding the ethics of corporate medicine requires analysis of the cultural, practical, and social constraints that are intrinsic to the work setting.

Medical programs first were established by companies in forestry, mining, and railroading to provide rudimentary medical services in remote areas. Between 1900 and 1920, they were introduced into industries with the purpose of screening workers to ensure high labor efficiency and to reduce absenteeism. Whereas the early company doctors saw themselves as delivering useful medical services, workers from the beginning viewed them as a threat.[19] Today, about 4,000 occupational physicians and 20,000 industrial nurses are employed directly by industry. They mainly work in large firms; 81% of companies with more than 50,000 workers have at least one full-time M.D., and many have large medical departments. DuPont, for example, employs 70 full-time and 50 part-time physicians and 2,000 registered nurses in its various plants throughout the United States.[20]

Company doctors are themselves employees; their company determines their wages and the conditions of their employment. Their benefits sometimes include stock holdings. Some doctors are formally a part of management, sometimes working as vice presidents for health.

The work of corporate physicians includes both medical and administrative tasks. They are responsible for preemployment screening of job applicants, routine examinations of workers to monitor any changes in their health, emergency care and referrals to specialized doctors, and evaluations of illnesses and complaints. In addition, occupational physicians have many administrative tasks. They collect and interpret data on the general level of health and safety in the plant, maintaining records on individual workers and on the entire workforce. Some are engaged in epidemiological studies. They also act as advisors to management, reporting on matters of health and safety. And they are called upon to testify in worker compensation cases, representing the company whenever there are disputes about whether an illness is associated with work. They not only provide health care services but practice what Diana Chapman Walsh has called "medical adjudication," evaluating medical fitness for promotions, eligibility for insurance, responsibility in tort liability cases, and justification for absences from work.[21]

These tasks often are straightforward when the problems involve accidents or obvious physical disabilities. The occupational physician's job, however, has been enormously complicated by the increasing problems arising from the proliferation of chemicals in the workplace. Many doctors are inadequately trained in the unique health problems involved in this growing area. Complaints often are vague, ambiguous, and difficult to interpret. Their judgments take place in a context of technical uncertainty that limits a precise interpretation of symptoms and precludes the definitive association of illness with work.[22] The effect of chronic exposure to chemicals may become evident only after a latency period of many years. The cumulative impact of prolonged exposure to low doses of certain chemicals and the synergistic effect of exposure to combinations of substances confound systematic evaluation. Moreover, many of the diagnostic techniques in this field are primitive and past records are inadequate to assist in the evaluation of complaints.

Technical uncertainty and the inadequacy of records leave open broad possibilities for interpretation. How does one evaluate vague symptoms? When should the worker be informed of potential hazards? When the technical bases for such decisions are poorly defined, the independent subjective judgment of the physician assumes increased importance.

The uncertainties inherent in the nature of this field of medicine are compounded by the ambiguities inherent in the corporate physician's role. The company doctor has two clients: the worker and the corporation. Bertram D. Dinman, M.D., states this explicitly when he talks of the corporation as "the patient":

> I would posit that not only may our patient be an actual flesh and blood person, but also that legal fiction of person, the body corporate. ... If the occupational physician considers both the individual and the corporation as his patient, his course should be set by a modification of the Hippocratic Oath that I would propose: "The regime I adopt shall be for the benefit of my patients, *Corporeal* and *Corporate*."[23]

Yet these two "patients" have very different goals. The corporation is under economic pressure to maintain productivity and profits, a goal that can conflict with the costly expenditures required to protect worker health. Whereas industry is concerned about the employees' fitness to work, workers are concerned about the fitness of the workplace and its effect on their health. The conflict becomes most explicit in worker compensation suits, when company physicians assume their administrative and adjudicatory role.

Worker compensation programs are designed to provide benefits and medical care for those with job-related injuries or disease.[24] Prior to the establishment of workers' compensation systems in the early part of the twentieth century, common law made it difficult for workers to sue their employers and win. Political pressure then led to reforms of state laws that facilitated workers' claims. In response, industry helped to create a system of compensation that would substitute a predictable administrative program for the increasingly risky decisions of the courts. In exchange for their right to sue their employer, workers gained social insurance against workplace accidents without regard to fault.

The compensation system was established primarily to deal with workplace injuries. It has many weaknesses when applied to occupational disease. Although the worker does not have to prove the company is at fault in a compensation claim, the problem does have to originate in or be aggravated by the workplace. Given the uncertain origins of many occupational health problems, compensation boards tend to be biased against such claims. Surveys suggest that only 2 to 3% of those reporting work-related disease, as against 38 to 43% reporting injuries, receive compensation. Of 1.8 million disability awards in 1975, only 1.7% were for illness. These cases are simply more easily contested than injury or accident claims.

Employers have a significant stake in contesting claims, and they use their medical departments to help them. Large firms that insure themselves have an obvious conflict of interest in evaluating claims for compensation. In most states companies purchase insurance from profit-motivated private carriers who want to minimize payouts. The insurance premiums are experience-rated; higher claims mean higher costs. To keep insurance costs down, company managers, with the help of their doctors, try to dismiss complaints as unrelated to work.[25]

Some corporations provide guidelines to their medical departments to guard against potential claims. These set out the terms under which medical personnel must operate. The concern about compensation claims is evident in an instruction manual for medical personnel at Standard Oil of Indiana—a company that in 1973 employed 45 health and safety specialists, including 8 physicians. The *Medical Manual* reads as follows:

> Any employee alleging an industrial injury will be asked to fill out, if he has not already done so, a "Report of Accident Form." He will be seen

by a company physician who will, in addition to examining the patient, take a careful history of matters having possible bearing on the complaint: a copy of the medical department report will be sent to the Claims Attorney.

In any questionable case, or in any case in which referral to an outside physician appears to be indicated, the Claims Attorney will be contacted by telephone while the patient is still in the Medical Department. The Claims Attorney and physician will discuss the case and agree on a course of action. No referrals will be made to an outside physician before contacting the Claims Attorney.[26]

While ethical guidelines call for confidentiality in the doctor-patient relationship, corporate constraints in this case require the intervention of a lawyer whenever there are medical complaints. Clearly, the norms of confidentiality guiding the physician in his or her role as healer are meaningless when the physician as record keeper becomes responsible to disclose information in the interests of the firm.

The *Medical Manual* insists that concern about costs also must enter the physician's medical judgment about when workers are well enough to return to work:

Because claims cases and absences from work due to real or alleged occupational injuries and illnesses are a significant cost item for the company, the medical department will evaluate such cases critically and frequently as to their ability to return to work, and approve them to do so as soon as possible.[27]

The manual goes on to note that "all claims cases are adversary cases and the comments of company physicians to employees must be guarded as to causation." This directive, following from concerns about possible financial liability, places limits on "timely and effective" communication of information as required by the physicians' ethical code. Identifying all compensation cases as adversarial, the statement belies the usual assertions about the confluence of interest concerning worker health.

These institutional constraints on the practice of corporate medicine are reinforced by a distinct set of cultural biases. These include ideas about the nature and seriousness of workplace risks.

Corporate publications tend to portray workplace hazards as minimal and acceptable. They often label people who worry about hazards as misinformed, emotional, and irrational. The fear of chemicals is framed in pathological terms as "chemophobia" or "cancerphobia." For example, the president of Monsanto is quoted in an article in *Nation's Business*: "The United States is suffering from an advanced case of chemophobia, an almost irrational fear of the products of chemistry."[28] A doctor, quoted in the business publication *Forbes*, denigrates workers' fears:

> Many people view cancer the way they viewed sex in old Broadway melodramas: As soon as a woman had her first sexual experience, she was pregnant. One whiff of a carcinogen and you have cancer.[29]

The corporation also frames the issue of risk in economic terms, emphasizing the need to make "reasonable" cost-benefit choices in protecting worker health. The culture is one of efficiency: Risks cannot be eliminated, only reduced to levels that are acceptable within a calculation of reasonable costs.

Finally, the cultural biases of industry equate industrial interests with the public interest. Operating from a world view that assumes consensus among major interests, industry advocates' public statements are punctuated with the pronouns "we" and "our."[30] Industry rejects the idea that workers may have different goals or that the profit motive can lead to neglect of workers' health. As *Nation's Business* put it, industry has "profit incentive" to protect workers and therefore acts in ways to "reduce the disease rate to the lowest level consistent with an efficient allocation of resources."[31]

This, then, is the context in which corporate physicians make medical and administrative judgments concerning the nature, origins, and reasonableness of workers' complaints. It is a context in which persistent technical uncertainties about the sources of occupational disease preclude rigorous medical decisions, leaving wide scope for personal judgments. It is a context in which the economic and social realities of professional work—the terms of work and cultural biases—raise questions about the relevance of scientific protocols.

The social context also leads us to wonder about the meaning of professional ethics. Can company doctors in fact observe the professional norms and implement the good intentions posited in ethical guidelines? These guidelines of occupational medicine were derived from the traditional fee-for-service relationship between the doctor in private practice and the individual patient. They reflect conditions of medical practice that encouraged an identity of interests between doctors and patients and, therefore, a relationship based on trust. In the context of corporate medicine, this relationship does not prevail: Thus, mistrust consistently is expressed by the workers who use corporate medical services.

The conflicting pressures confronting the company doctor are evident, but they are not unique. Similar dilemmas are intrinsic to a growing number of medical settings.[32] The problem of dual loyalties has long been present in a number of specialized contexts, such as sports teams, prisons, the military, and drug clinics. But physicians today also are increasingly employed by insurance companies, private hospitals, and other institutions that supply or pay for health care for a profit.[33] These are institutions in which doctors are necessarily judged by standards enforced by their occupational association, in which their professional loyalties may conflict with their organization's demands. The workers' mistrust of company doctors portends the kind of conflicts that are likely to accompany the growth of the large, profit-based health care institutions. For in such settings, the organization of medical practice, as well as the salaries and the careers of practitioners, may depend more on the priorities of their patrons than on the satisfaction of their patients.

NOTES

1. Norbert J. Roberts, "Ethical Issues in Occupational Medicine," New York Academy of Medicine *Bulletin* 54 (September 1978): 706.

2. Sheldon Samuels, cited in the *Wall Street Journal*, 8 October 1975.

3. See the arguments advanced by Eliot Freidson, *Professional Dominance* (New York: Atherton Press, 1970).

4. American Occupational Medical Association, *Code of Ethical Conduct*, adopted 23 July 1976.

5. For a review of legal standards, see Glen Provost and Edward Richards, "The Company Doctor's Responsibility to the Employee," *Trial* 17 (July 1981): 35-37; and George Annas, "Legal Aspects of Medical Confidentiality in the Occupational Setting," *Journal of Occupational Medicine* 18 (August 1976): 532-540.

6. Irving Tabershaw, "Whose Agent is the Occupational Physician?" *Archives of Environmental Health* 30 (1975): 412-416.

7. Parry M. Norling, "Health and Safety in the Chemical Industry" (Paper given at the Chemical Industry Seminar for the Office of Pesticides and Toxic Substances, U.S. Environmental Protection Agency, May 14, 1980), p. 1.

8. These assumptions about consensus are developed by Stephen Hilgartner in Chapter 2 of this volume. The physicians' adoption of these assumptions reflects a confusion between managerial and medical roles. This is described by Diana Chapman Walsh and Janet K. Marantz, "The Roles of the Corporate Medical Director," in *Industry and Health Care I*, eds. Richard Egdahl and Diana C. Walsh (Cambridge, MA: Ballinger, 1983). Also see Diana Chapman Walsh, "The Corporate Medical Quandry," *Business and Health*, June 1984, pp. 27-31.

9. Robert R. Hilker, cited in "New Corporate Physician," *Impact*, 12 November 1979, p. 6.

10. Bernard D. Dinman, "The Loyalty of the Occupational Physician," New York Academy of Medicine *Bulletin* 54 (September 1978): 729-732.

11. Bruce W. Karrh, "A Company's Duty to Report Health Hazards," New York Academy of Medicine *Bulletin* 54 (September 1978): 783.

12. James Spraul, lecture at Hastings Center Conference on Divided Loyalties in Medicine, December 10, 1981.

13. Neil Friedman, *The Social Nature of Psychological Research* (New York: Basic Books, 1967), p. 142.

14. Vivienne Walters, "Company Doctors' Perception of and Response to Conflicting Pressure From Labor and Management," *Social Problems* 30 (October 1982): 1-12.

15. The following quotes are from workers interviewed as part of our NSF-funded project on workers' attitudes toward risk. See Dorothy Nelkin and Michael S. Brown, *Workers at Risk: Voices From the Workplace* (Chicago: University of Chicago Press, 1984).

16. "Medical Exams are First Weapon in Protecting You in the Workplace," *The Chemical Worker*, September 1982, p. 9.

17. Eliot Freidson, *Profession of Medicine* (New York: Dodd Mead, 1970), p. 367.

18. Mary Douglas, "Cultural Bias" (London, Royal Anthropological Society occasional paper 34). See also Mary Douglas and Aaron Wildavsky, *Risk and Culture* (Berkeley: University of California Press, 1982).

19. Analla Nugent, "Fit for Work: The Introduction of Physical Examination in Industry," *Bulletin of the History of Medicine*, Winter 1983, pp. 578-595.

20. DuPont Employee Relations Department, *Occupational Medicine Program* (Wilmington, DE: DuPont, 1981).

21. Diana Chapman Walsh, "Is There a Doctor In-House," *Harvard Business Review* 4 (July-August 1984): 84-94.

22. A standard reference on industrial toxicology and occupational disease is F. A. Patty, *Patty's Industrial Hygiene and Toxicology*, eds. G. D. Clayton and F. E. Clayton, 3 vol. (New York: John Wiley, 1978). For general background, see Jeanne Stellman and Susan Daum, *Work is Dangerous to Your Health* (New York: Vintage Books, 1973).

23. Dinman, "Loyalty of the Physician," 1978.

24. Peter S. Barth and H. Allan Hunt, *Workers Compensation and Work-Related Illnesses and Diseases* (Cambridge, MA: MIT Press, 1980).

25. Only 2 to 3% of those reporting work-related disease, as against 38 to 43% of those reporting injuries, receive compensation. Health complaints are simply easier to contest.

26. Standard Oil Company of Indiana, *Medical Manual*, April 1972, quoted in Michael Berman, *Death on the Job* (New York: Monthly Review Press, 1978), pp. 108-109.

27. Ibid., p. 109.

28. Michael Thoryn, "Chemicals and Plastics: The Catalysts of Living," *Nation's Business*, March 1979, p. 70.

29. "Diseased Regulation," *Forbes*, February 1979, p. 34.

30. For a comparison of consensus and conflict models of society, see Thomas J. Bernard, *The Consensus/Conflict Debate* (New York: Columbia University Press, 1983). Also see Hilgartner, Chapter 2 of this volume.

31. Barry Crickmer, "Regulation: How Much is Enough?" *Nation's Business*, March 1980, p. 29.

32. Michael Betz and Lenahan O'Connell, "Company Doctor-Patient Relationships and the Rise in Concern for Accountability," *Social Problems* 31 (1973): 84-95.

33. Arnold S. Relman, "The New Medical Industrial Complex," *New England Journal of Medicine* 303 (1980): 963-970.

5

THE MISRULE OF LAW AT OSHA

Sheila Jasanoff

France has its *grand corps* of administrators and Britain its esteemed generalist civil servants. Those who deplore the absence of comparable professional cadres in the United States overlook the fact that administrative processes in this country derive from an equally powerful culture, that of lawyers and the courts. Since the earliest days of the American administrative state, each cycle of concern about the runaway power of the bureaucracy has generated reforms rooted in legal concepts: the rule of law, separation of powers, due process, judicial review. To circumscribe the discretionary authority of regulatory agencies, the federal government has developed a body of legal requirements that dwarf the administrative law codes of continental Europe. Particularly in the 1970s, legalism was carried to extraordinary lengths in a spate of new regulatory statutes. Congress not only imposed more rigorous rule-making procedures on the agencies, but greatly expanded the public's right to challenge the agencies in court. Concern about overregulation in the 1980s brought further demands for legally enforceable controls on government, including mandatory cost-benefit analysis, risk assessment, and scientific peer review.

Conceived and implemented by lawyers, administrative decision making in the United States is stamped with the

distinctive procedural hallmarks of litigation: open and adversarial argument, preparation of elaborate technical "cases,"
and a delegation of ultimate responsibility for resolving conflicts to the courts. These features frequently have been criticized for making the regulatory process cumbersome, costly,
and divisive.[1] Yet Congress never has deviated from the position that strict procedural controls and judicial review are the
best means of holding administrators publicly accountable.

In this chapter I examine the regulatory record of the Occupational Safety and Health Administration (OSHA) since the
mid-1970s and argue that formal procedures have not, in fact,
promoted greater accountability in that agency's decision making. OSHA's history during the past decade reveals a reality
very much at odds with the ideal of the rule of law. Procedures
adopted to ensure the legitimacy of administrative action not
only have created delay and uncertainty but have failed to
provide adequate safeguards against incompetence and bad
faith. Adversarial processes have forced both OSHA and concerned private groups to develop polarized positions, under-
cutting the prospects for fruitful negotiation. Open rule making has undermined public confidence in the agency by
exposing the discretionary character of its decisions and the
absence of any compelling logic for particular policy choices.

OSHA's experience suggests that the litigation model for
framing and resolving regulatory dilemmas is particularly ill-
suited to dealing with problems of scientific uncertainty. The
adversarial methods of the law, with their emphasis on "finding
facts" and establishing "truth," provide little guidance in situations in which even experts agree that there is no clearly right
answer. Moreover, in applying the rationalistic legal approach
to evaluating scientific data, agencies overlook the fact that
such information is the product of independent social and
cultural processes, with their own more subtle rules for pro-
moting legitimacy. In the drive to meet standards of legal
decision making, administrators lose sight of the standards by
which the scientific community establishes the quality and

credibility of information. In OSHA's case, this insensitivity has fed the perception among scientists that agency officials are not interested in "good science," but are prepared to allow political considerations to override any consensus among experts.

An analysis of OSHA's major regulatory proceedings also shakes one's faith in the efficacy of judicial review as a technique for controlling agency discretion. Although passing on the legal validity of specific decisions, courts have failed to address the generic shortcomings of OSHA's administrative process. In the most controversial cases, the courts have found it difficult to disentangle legal and factual issues or to identify the most serious deficiencies in the agency's reasoning. Judges have been hampered by a lack of technical expertise in evaluating the contradictory arguments advanced by labor and industry. Judicial decisions have been inconsistent across jurisdictions and over time, adding to the confusion and ambiguity surrounding OSHA's legal mandate.

Problems such as these are unknown in other advanced industrial nations, where one finds an approach to legitimating administrative decisions that is radically different from this country's law-obsessed vision.[2] Instead of controlling discretion by legal mechanisms—through mandatory procedures, reporting, disclosure requirements, and judicial review—these countries attempt to constrain discretion by less formal means. They rely more on cultural than procedural controls. European governments, for example, have sought to legitimate their regulatory policies by building up bureaucratic and technical expertise in the executive branch and by shielding civil servants from the pressures of partisan politics. Working through consultation and negotiation, European decision makers prevent the polarization of divergent viewpoints and encourage consensus building. Scientific judgments, in particular, are developed through private deliberations among experts, so that expert disagreements are not exposed to public view. Although decisions are made behind closed doors, the public's trust in the legitimacy of administrative action is maintained through institutional stability and the assurance that the rules of the regulatory game will not change drastically with changes in political leadership.

In recent years, a growing number of comparative policy studies have urged that American decision makers should give serious thought to the virtues of the less formal and legalistic European regulatory approach.[3] These recommendations are based on cross-national comparisons suggesting that, particularly in the area of chemical regulation, European governments have adopted standards comparable to those in the United States, but with considerably lower expenditures of time and resources. European chemical control policies also have displayed greater consistency in priority setting and in overall regulatory philosophy than have U.S. policies during the past decade. These observations provide compelling grounds for questioning the effectiveness of the American approach to regulation.

But reform proposals based on comparative analysis tend to underestimate the extent to which U.S. policy making is shaped by the dynamics of the legal process. In OSHA's case, for example, the dominance of the legal culture seems to have undercut efforts to develop a self-regulatory administrative ethos. Thus, although OSHA's record underscores the urgency of institutional and procedural reform, it also suggests that fundamental changes will be difficult to achieve, particularly in the direction of informal, consultative decision making. After discussing some of the social and political factors that preserve the appeal of the litigation model in the United States, I argue that administrative reform in this country can be undertaken successfully only if we make some basic changes in the perspectives that lawyers, who dominate the regulatory process, bring to the task of public administration.

RULE MAKING AND SCIENTIFIC UNCERTAINTY

During the Carter years, OSHA's primary emphasis was on the regulation of occupational carcinogens. Two major policy initiatives—the development of a new exposure limit for benzene and the formulation of a generic "cancer policy"—consumed most of the agency's resources in this period. Neither effort led to enforceable results, primarily because of OSHA's failure to find stable compromises on scientific issues. Examining these cases in detail tells us a great deal about the hazards of attempting to build a scientific consensus exclusively through the rules of the legal process.

OSHA's decision to begin rule making on benzene reflected the Carter administration's activist orientation on health and safety policy. Assistant Secretary Eula Bingham came to her post with a commitment to "do something" about occupational health, a problem OSHA consistently underemphasized in relation to safety issues throughout the early 1970s. A frequent complaint against the agency in the Nixon and Ford years was its slow pace of rule making on major health hazards, especially occupational carcinogens.[4] Benzene, one of the ten largest volume industrial chemicals in use today, was convincingly linked to human leukemia in the early 1970s. It seemed an ideal regulatory target for an agency anxious to enhance its reputation and impact. Indeed, by the time Bingham's appointment was announced, rubber and plastics workers already had petitioned OSHA to reduce the exposure limit below 10 ppm. Bingham's own professional experience with occupational illness in the Ohio rubber industry also predisposed her to use benzene as the test case for a tougher policy on carcinogens.

With a major policy objective charted out in advance, the agency turned to its enabling legislation for the quickest means of achieving its ends. The obvious solution was to proceed

under Section 6(c) of the Occupational Safety and Health Act
(OSH Act), a provision that permits the bypassing of more
rigorous due process requirements when there is "grave
danger" to employees from a toxic agent in the workplace. The
6(c) procedure also offered important symbolic benefits. An
emergency temporary standard (ETS) taking speedy effect
would send a strong signal to industry about OSHA's intention
to crack down on carcinogens. Science presented the only
serious obstacle. Some agency officials believed that the
evidence on benzene was not strong enough to support the
drastic action authorized by Section 6(c). They argued in
particular that there was no new information suggesting a risk
to workers at exposure levels below the existing standard.
Their reservations persuaded the assistant secretary that more
evidence was needed, but did not deter her from proceeding
under Section 6(c). Even before Bingham assumed office,
events were set in motion to generate scientific results consistent with the administration's desire for rapid action.

Under pressure to produce such data, experts at the
National Institute for Occupational Safety and Health
(NIOSH) responded with what observers have described as
"mail-order science," reporting evidence of leukemia among
rubber workers at significantly lower levels of exposure than
previously recorded. On the strength of these findings, OSHA
announced an ETS of 1 ppm in April 1977. However, as the
standard-setting process unfolded and the NIOSH data were
subjected to outside scientific review, the agency's methodology and results increasingly came under fire, forcing OSHA to
retreat from the position that there was direct epidemiological
support for the 1 ppm standard. The effect on OSHA's scientific credibility was deplorable. The incident not only embar-
rassed the agency, but provided excellent ammunition for
chemical companies, which had been arguing for some time
that the agencies were not competent to be entrusted with
scientific decision making.[5]

Ultimately, the legal framework that permitted OSHA to go
forward with questionable scientific data also provided the

means to stop the agency. The controversial ETS was caught up in litigation and never enforced. Moreover, OSHA's awkward efforts to distance itself from the NIOSH study undermined its credibility and played an important part in the Supreme Court's decision to invalidate the 1 ppm standard eventually promulgated by the agency. But these results hold at best cold comfort for supporters of the adjudicatory approach to decision making. The process as a whole "worked" in the sense that OSHA was not allowed to get away with an abuse of discretion. But the final result was to throw the baby out with the bath water. The Supreme Court's verdict invalidated a control measure that many experts, both inside and outside the chemical industry, regarded not merely as necessary but also as feasible and effective. The negative court judgment also forced the agency to go back to square one, thereby ensuring no return to workers from OSHA's substantial investment in the benzene rule making.

While benzene was being regulated with the fanfare due to an important test case, OSHA embarked on a still more ambitious effort to develop a generic "cancer policy." This comprehensive body of rules was to provide the agency a secure legal basis for its future efforts to control carcinogens. The agency's perception of the relevant scientific issues, its choice of "solutions," and its strategy for achieving the desired goal can be understood only as products of a legalistic culture. To begin with, OSHA's main reason for adopting a "cancer policy" was to avoid the recurrent litigation surrounding federal attempts to regulate carcinogens. The agency proposed to do this by resolving through policy guidelines the scientific issues that were most frequently debated in regulatory and judicial proceedings, such as the design and interpretation of animal experiments, the relevance of negative epidemiological data, and the existence of "safe" exposure thresholds for carcinogens. The decision to cast the cancer policy in the form of binding regulations also reflected legal norms of accountability. It is a dominant principle of American administrative law that agencies should engage in rule making wherever possible in order to exercise in a principled way the large discretion conferred on them by Congress.[6]

In developing the scientific foundation of the cancer policy OSHA conscientiously followed the judicialized procedures of "hybrid" rule making. The agency heard evidence from some 54 witnesses representing the major concerned interest groups: industry, labor, environmental groups, and government science. The record of the hearings, together with written submissions, added up to more than a quarter million pages. This approach was thoroughly successful in spotting the important scientific issues and illuminating the areas of disagreement among experts. But the process failed to provide something far more important: a unified theory of risk assessment commanding substantial public support. The decision to conceptualize carcinogen regulation as a "generic" problem—a decision driven by concern about litigation—led to enormous technical and political difficulties. Many of the scientific questions addressed by OSHA proved difficult, if not impossible, to answer at a generic level. In addition, the high stakes associated with a single, generic approach to regulating *all* occupational carcinogens hardened the positions of both industry and labor, so that OSHA was forced to make seemingly arbitrary choices between extreme and irreconcilable positions.

The formal rules of administrative decision making gave OSHA little guidance on how to proceed in these difficult circumstances. Under prevailing legal doctrines, OSHA was required to take a "hard look" at the evidence before it and to make a "reasoned decision" consistent with its overall statutory mandate. As the length of the hearing record demonstrates, OSHA took these standards of conduct at face value and expended enormous effort in trying to live up to them. The cancer policy as finally promulgated was reasoned in the sense that it was accompanied by detailed technical explanations. Yet it ultimately failed because it seriously misunderstood the way in which scientists evaluate data, particularly in the highly judgmental sphere of risk assessment.

OSHA proposed a rather crude metric for resolving the expert differences revealed during the cancer policy hearing. Briefly, in each case in which scientific theory or evidence indicated that it was possible to draw more than one plausible inference, OSHA selected the most "conservative" or most "pro-health" option. Put differently, OSHA's policy intentionally produced the largest number of false positives, a result OSHA justified in terms of its legal mandate to reduce occupational risk to the lowest feasible extent. Many of OSHA's determinations, however, are more difficult to explain in scientific terms.[7] For example, the agency indicated that it always would give preference to positive animal tests over nonpositive epidemiological studies. To effectuate this policy, OSHA proposed to exclude all negative epidemiological evidence from its deliberations unless the studies conformed to standards that are almost impossible to meet given the state of the art in cancer epidemiology. Many reputable scientists agreed with OSHA that positive animal tests should be given greater weight than negative epidemiological studies where public health is at stake, but few were prepared to accept a scheme that completely ruled out negative epidemiological information, particularly as a factor to consider in quantitative risk assessment. Indeed, in the view of many experts, the policy of absolute exclusion destroyed the validity of OSHA's entire approach to risk assessment.

Ironically, portions of the cancer policy even seem inadequate by the criterion of reasoned decision making that the agency accepted as controlling. The threshold criteria for screening nonpositive epidemiological studies are an example. OSHA adopted these criteria at a late stage in the proceedings, as a device for excluding evidence that it did not wish to rebut in later case-by-case decisions on specific substances. As a result, the hearing record contained no discussion relating to such criteria. Participants in the rule-making process had no opportunity to comment on either the general advisability of such screening rules or the technical merit of the particular standards the agency proposed to apply. As in the benzene case, formal compliance with administrative procedures did not lead to a decision based entirely on the public record. The instrumental use of procedure in both cases to advance the agency's preconceived policy goals reveals the inadequacy of formal rule making as a technique for limiting administrative discretion.

JUDICIAL REVIEW:
TOO LITTLE, TOO LATE

Recourse to the courts always has been the proper remedy for private individuals injured by unlawful government action. In the U.S. administrative process, however, courts have a role going well beyond the protection of private rights. Regulatory statutes such as the OSH Act are freighted with detailed procedural requirements, timetables, and nondiscretionary duties, all of which can be enforced by the courts. To ensure that administrators will be answerable to the courts, Congress also has systematically reduced the standing barriers to suits against government agencies, so that private citizens often have a right of action though they have no personal stake in the challenged regulatory proceedings. Support for strict judicial supervision of the administrative agencies remains high, even in the Reagan administration. In 1982, for example, a Republican Senate approved a bill instructing judges not to defer to agency interpretations of law.[8] The provision was designed to give the courts a still larger voice in shaping regulatory policy. Coming at a time of general public disenchantment with the courts, the proposal was a powerful reminder that American politicians and policy makers, regardless of their political affiliations, unquestioningly accept judicial review as the primary defense against abuses of administrative discretion.

The record of OSHA's relations with the courts indicates that such pervasive trust in the corrective effects of judicial review may be misplaced, particularly when courts are required to review agency decisions based on complex technical information. A frequent judicial response in such cases is reluctance to exercise independent critical judgment, a posture that courts justify by deferring to the agency's special technical expertise. For example, until the benzene decision, OSHA's standards for occupational carcinogens routinely were upheld, so that the early cases provide few indications that courts are institutionally capable of circumscribing agency discretion. The courts consistently adopted a tough stand toward the agency in only one subgroup of cases, those involving emergency temporary standards (ETS). Litigation, not always leading to a final decision on the merits, prevented enforcement of the ETSs for benzene, 14 organic chemicals, and, most recently, asbestos. But in these cases the key questions before the court were relatively nontechnical. The basic issue was the legality of the expedited rule-making procedure, and courts were confronted with the relatively unproblematic task of determining whether the agency had a valid reason for acting in the "emergency" mode. In deciding whether the information on which the agency acted was sufficient to justify emergency action, judges did not have to undertake a searching review of a detailed technical record.

In the case involving the regular occupational safety and health standard for benzene, however, both the Fifth Circuit and the Supreme Court were asked to consider whether the proposed exposure limit of 1 ppm was supported by a rational and well-reasoned assessment of risk to exposed workers. The lower court chose not to address the issue of risk directly, electing instead to reject the standard because of the agency's failure to perform cost-benefit analysis.[9] In the Supreme Court, however, a majority of the justices did not see cost-benefit analysis as the central issue in the case.[10] Nevertheless, one member of the court, Justice Rehnquist, believed that the case could be decided without reference to the standard's scientific validity. Rehnquist reasoned that the provision under which the benzene standard was promulgated was too vague to provide adequate guidance to the agency. He therefore held that the statutory provision should be invalidated as an unconstitutional delegation of legislative power. By resurrecting this almost forgotten doctrine of administrative law, Rehnquist successfully evaded the technical arguments advanced by the petroleum industry.

The remaining eight members of the court grappled with the scientific issues, but with only limited success. Four justices reviewed the decision-making record in detail and concluded that OSHA had taken the required "hard look" at the information before it and had provided "substantial evidence" to support the proposed standard. If this view had prevailed, it would have prevented a substantial waste of public resources and let stand a decision that was arguably "right" as a matter of health and safety. Yet OSHA would not have been held accountable for its questionable decision to ignore industry's claims about risk at low levels of benzene exposure. By not responding to industry's risk assessment, OSHA was hoping to establish the principle that it is unnecessary to quantify risk in developing exposure standards. This position was consistent with OSHA's overall aim of streamlining the rule-making process and preserving its own maneuvering room. But in failing to answer a major industry argument, OSHA violated the cardinal principle of reasoned decision-making: that agencies should consider and respond to all significant issues raised by affected interests. The dissenting justices suggested no penalty for this violation.

The plurality's analysis of the case, though reasonable in several particulars, does not generate much greater confidence in the corrective power of judicial review. Given the gaps in OSHA's record, the justices certainly were on firm ground in asking the agency to make a threshold showing of "significant" risk to workers at the existing standard of 10ppm. This demand not only was responsive to industry's claims concerning risk assessment, but was consistent with the established legal principle that governmental power should not be invoked against negligible or *de minimis* risks.[11] Following this doctrine, regulation cannot be justified merely by the presence of harmful substances in the workplace, but only by the discovery of a real or significant threat to the health and safety of exposed individuals. The plurality's dissatisfaction with the overall quality of OSHA's reasoning also was understandable, as the agency never fully explained its abandonment of one scientific rationale (the disputed epidemiological evidence of cancer at low exposure levels) for another (theoretical arguments indicating no safe threshold of exposure to carcinogens). In asking the agency to express its scientific arguments more clearly and cogently, the court was exercising the kind of control we legitimately expect from a technically untrained judiciary.

A more troublesome aspect of the plurality opinion was the attempt to give operational meaning to legal concepts such as de minimis risk and substantial evidence. In discussing the validity of the proposed 1 ppm standard, the plurality attached great weight to the "sketchiness" of the administrative record with respect to the adverse effects of low-level exposure to benzene. To correct this, the court demanded "evidence" of a significant risk at existing occupational exposures and strongly suggested that the agency should construct a plausible dose-response curve in order to meet this evidentiary obligation. OSHA and its fellow regulatory agencies interpreted the opinion as a judicial mandate to perform quantitative risk assessments in regulating carcinogens and other hazardous substances. Yet opinion in the scientific community remains deeply divided about the validity of such assessments under present conditions of uncertainty. Toxicologists, in particular, note with dismay that the fit between mathematical extrapolations of risk and data from animal experiments frequently is poor. Statistical models, in their view, often are flawed because they rest on only limited understanding of the biological processes by which chemicals induce disease in test animals. Moreover, the pressure to produce quantitative estimates, coupled with a disregard for experimental findings, can drive the agencies to insupportable manipulations of data, such as constructing an entire dose-response curve on the basis of a single data point.

In spite of the Supreme Court's endorsement, risk assessment thus remains a highly inexact, even questionable "science." In future cases even industry may argue that the procedure is too deeply flawed to serve as a useful analytical tool.

To be sure, ambiguities in the benzene decision cast doubt on the rigidity of the court's command to perform quantitative risk assessments. For example, the court noted at one point that "the requirement that a 'significant' risk be identified is not a mathematical straitjacket."[12] The statement implies that quantification is not necessarily a precondition to regulating risk. The court also acknowledged that "there are a number of ways in which the agency can make a rational judgment about the relative significance of the risks associated with exposure to a particular carcinogen." This means that agencies retain some discretion in their choice of risk assessment methodologies. However, read in the context of the actual dispute between the petroleum industry and OSHA, the benzene case leaves little doubt that the Supreme Court's sympathies lay with quantitative analysis of risk. In the end, this judicial preference is troubling because it seems clear that the court's views were based on an imperfect understanding of the scientific arguments surrounding risk assessment. Indeed, many now believe that a Supreme Court ruling in favor of quantitative risk assessment was premature and ill-advised.

The history of OSHA's relations with the courts highlights another danger of relying too heavily on judicial review to correct abuses of administrative discretion. As OSHA's record shows, the need to supervise the agencies is strongest at the earliest stages of the policy process, where goals are identified, research is commissioned, and decisions are made about the choice of analytical techniques and control instruments. Yet courts have no opportunity to comment on these basic policy choices until the end of a long and divisive regulatory proceeding. The formal procedures imposed on the agencies by Congress and the courts ensure that years will elapse and thousands of pages of evidence be developed between an agency's initial strategic decisions and the commencement of judicial review.

At such a late date, faced with records of overwhelming complexity, judges find it almost impossible to identify the real fault lines in the administrative process or the most significant breaks in the agency's reasoning. Moreover, the sheer weight of the technical record shapes each case into a unique pattern that is difficult to review in terms of general legal principles. As in the benzene case, judges frequently cannot agree either about the rationale for invalidating a decision or about the proper remedy. Finally, by the time a judicial opinion is handed down, the cast of characters in the agency is so thoroughly altered that the prospect of administrators learning anything from judicial review becomes almost illusory.

LAWYERS AS BUREAUCRATS

The movement toward regulatory reform in the Carter and Reagan administrations generated expectations that the excessively legalistic and cumbersome American administrative process might be modified in the direction of the more flexible European approach. Management considerations were to replace ideology and a more routinized, orderly process was to substitute for seemingly unlimited litigation and technical controversy. OSHA's activities during the first Reagan term show that the reality has been different. Ideological motivations have continued to take precedence over managerial considerations, and the agency has failed to break away from the adversarial, winner-take-all ethic of the legal process.

An incident in the early years of the Reagan administration illustrates how deeply the adversarial spirit permeates American agencies. This was the attempted firing of Dr. Peter Infante, one of the scientists responsible for the controversial study of rubber workers' exposure to benzene and a well-known spokesman for a tough regulatory approach toward occupational carcinogens. The reason given for Infante's dismissal was consistent with the new OSHA administration's emphasis on sound management. Infante was charged with insubordination, in other words, a failure to conform to the norms of bureaucratic behavior. Specifically, Infante had written a letter to the International Agency for Research on Cancer (IARC) urging that agency to reconsider the information contained in a NIOSH Current Intelligence Bulletin (CIB) on formaldehyde. Just before the letter was written, Thorne Auchter, the Reagan-appointed OSHA head, had decided not to cosponsor the NIOSH CIB or formally endorse its contents. Infante's opponents argued that his continued public support for the CIB was in violation of expressed agency policy, as well as a misrepresentation of OSHA, as he wrote as an official, using OSHA letterhead.

Other facts, however, severely compromised the claim that OSHA was simply protecting the integrity of the administrative process. For example, a Congressional hearing on the proposed firing revealed that OSHA was influenced by complaints from the law firm representing the Formaldehyde Institute, the trade association for the formaldehyde industry. Moreover, Auchter's decision not to cosign the formaldehyde CIB was itself in conflict with established bureaucratic norms. The decision apparently was triggered by a deputation from the Formaldehyde Institute raising questions about the scientific quality of the NIOSH CIB. Under Congressional questioning, Auchter admitted that he consulted with his senior staff scientists, including Dr. Infante, before reaching the CIB decision. However, Auchter, not himself a trained scientist, went against the recommendations of his scientific staff in holding that OSHA should not publicly endorse the NIOSH document. To cover up this deviation from standard administrative practice, Auchter used a familiar rhetorical ploy. He characterized the CIB decision as "policy," not science, noting that "there is nobody responsible for policy in the agency but me." Infante, for his part, set this argument aside with the claim that he was acting in the interests of "science," not policy.

Despite attempts to treat it as a problem of bureaucratic discipline, the Infante incident was from start to finish an adversarial drama played out according to the rules of the courtroom. This was particularly evident during hearings held by a House subcommittee chaired by Congressman Gore. In a scene that would be unimaginable in a true administrative culture, Assistant Secretary Auchter appeared before the committee to answer the charges against him, characteristically accompanied by his counsel, the Deputy Solicitor of Labor, and his special assistant for regulatory affairs, another trained lawyer. The procedures and the rhetoric used by the participants all were appropriate to a trial setting, as illustrated by the following exchange between the committee chairman and the administrator:

> Mr. Auchter: Well, Mr. Chairman, believe me I would love to respond to your questions about the Dr. Infante situation. I cannot. I am precluded by our solicitor's office from doing that. I will be glad to come back and talk to you after it has been brought to its final conclusion through the appropriate process so that all parties are protected, not only Dr. Infante and the agency and Dr. Walker, but all the other career civil servants that we have, which is the reason for the Civil Service Act.
>
> We have a process to follow. We are going to follow it.
>
> Mr. Gore: Well, we have a process to follow, too, Mr. Auchter, and it is outlined in the Constitution of the United States. The Constitution of the United States gives the Congress the right to conduct oversight into the proceedings of the executive branch.[13]

It is hard to say which party here acted most in keeping with the culture of litigation: the administrator hiding a political decision behind an argument about proper procedures or the legislator pulling out the Constitution as the ultimate trump card in the debate.

OSHA rule-making activities during the Reagan administration, although less entertaining as public theater, also illustrate the generally detrimental impact of the adversarial legal culture on social regulation. The agency's record on ethylene oxide, a widely used sterilizing agent and fumigant, provides a

routine example. Evidence that ethylene oxide causes cancer in
humans led several unions and Nader's Public Citizen Health
Research Group to petition for a new exposure standard limiting workplace concentrations of the substance to 1 ppm.
OSHA's first response was no response, a favored strategy of
any agency that wishes not to decide. A few months after
turning away the labor and public interest petitioners, OSHA
announced that it would begin rule making on ethylene oxide,
but indicated that it would take at least three years to issue a
final rule. Impatient with this prognosis, the pro-regulation
groups followed the usual path and took the agency to court. A
federal district judge responded sympathetically, ordering
OSHA to issue an ETS for ethylene oxide. Subsequently, the
Court of Appeals for the District of Columbia slightly modified the order, holding that an ETS was not required, but that
the agency should stop its "unreasonable delay" and promulgate a new standard within a year.[14]

Decisions like this, in which a public interest group obtains
court-ordered action from an administrative agency, have
become increasingly common on the American regulatory
scene. They are cited by conservative political theorists as
illegitimate extensions of judicial power. Managing the timing
or flow of regulation, they contend, is a quintessentially executive function that should lie beyond the reach of judicial intervention. Yet the argument loses force when agencies repeatedly
hesitate or refuse to act except under pressure of lawsuit and
court order. This reluctance cuts across both liberal and conservative administrations. Federal bureaucrats often complain
that it is pointless and frustrating to develop long-range programs when the regulatory agenda really is determined by crisis
reports in the *Washington Post* and the *New York Times*. But
looking at the way agencies behave, one must conclude that
regulators depend at least as much on the courts as on the
media to prod them into action. It is as if administrators are
unwilling to treat any issue as really important unless someone
takes them to court over it. Yet the strategy of waiting for the
courts unites administrative agencies with the larger social

forces that expand judicial power and whittle away at the distinctions between judging and policy making in America.

At a less abstract level, OSHA's performance over the past decade illustrates the terrible inefficiency of the present judge-centered and adversarial regulatory process. The generic cancer policy, for example, consumed the lion's share of the agency resources for four years, but was set aside without a word of explanation after the 1980 election. Such waste seems intolerable from a management perspective, but with no continuity of leadership in the agencies, it is hard to see how anyone can be held accountable for mismanagement. Worse still, OSHA's subsequent attempts to regulate specific carcinogens, such as benzene, formaldehyde, asbestos, and ethylene oxide, show few conceptual or procedural advances that can be linked to the intellectual exercise undertaken by the agency in developing the cancer policy. The example of benzene is especially illuminating. Following the fiasco in the Supreme Court, OSHA sponsored a bargaining process between labor and industry to see whether it could achieve through negotiation what it had failed to get by litigation. Although the negotiations made considerable progress, narrowing the differences between the companies and the unions on many issues, the process eventually fell through. The petroleum industry attempted to use the negotiations as a vehicle for major changes in OSHA's enforcement policies, and labor became worried about the tentative agreement as a precedent in future rule making. Ultimately, the possibility of an accord was undercut by the distrust that predominates in a litigious environment, a factor that OSHA did not have the legal, political, or moral authority to overcome.

This is a distressing state of affairs, but it would be naive to expect anything different in a system that offers so few rewards for stability or compromise. Indeed, the incentives usually run the other way and, for administrators serving pitifully brief terms in the agencies, the prospect of winning political victories in the short term takes precedence over any more thoughtful or balanced vision of public policy.

THE APPEAL OF LAW

I have argued that elaborate standards, adversarial procedures, and judicial review add considerably to the cost and
complexity of regulatory programs; but they do not accom-
plish their intended function of securing impartial and rational
decisions. The evidence from OSHA's record, in particular, is
depressing, if not damning. If the ideal of lawful administration is so difficult to attain by means of legalistic techniques,
why do all political groups in America give their unswerving
allegiance to this model of decision making? Part of the answer
lies in the capacity of the legal process to serve two very
different social needs. To a people mistrustful of elites, the
European model of entrenched, expert bureaucracies carries
many negative connotations. Controlling administrative behavior through legal processes offers the possibility of impos-
ing a common standard on bureaucrats without creating special elites. It is an inherently democratic approach. Anyone,
regardless of prior training and experience, can be entrusted
with the task of public administration, as he or she will be
serving under law, constrained by formal procedures and the
watchful eye of the courts. Legal standards and rules convey a
sense of neutrality and permanence that one does not expect
from other human institutions. Both the concept of law and the
courts responsible for enforcing it are seen as standing above
and apart from politics. The notion of a "higher law" can be a
powerful rhetorical aid in politics, as Congressman Gore knew
when he reprimanded the OSHA assistant secretary by saying,
"Well, we have a process to follow, too, Mr. Auchter, and it is
outlined in the Constitution of the United States."

But the law is not merely an abstract concept. In the hands of
lawyers, it serves a pragmatic purpose, providing the technical
tools for winning cases. The instrumental functions of the law
are ideally suited to the politics of pluralism. Any interest
group, however powerless or disenfranchised in the arena of
national politics, can construct a favorable legal argument and

attempt to win in court what it could not gain through the political process. In fact, the trends in administrative law over the past 15 years—liberalized access, judicial review, freedom of information, funding for citizen intervenors—have encouraged greater recourse to the courts by redressing the balance of power among interest groups commanding very different resources. The committed public interest group and the large private corporation seem more nearly equal in court-like settings than in any other institutional forum. Advocates of firmer regulatory policy thus believe, with some justice, that their interests are better served by a litigation-oriented administrative process than by a less adversarial system, in which influence is exerted by hidden routes and it is harder to challenge the government's balancing of economic concerns against health, safety, and the quality of life.

CONCLUSION

The reliance on law to structure and legitimate administrative decisions is linked so closely to deeper social and political forces in America that it would be unproductive to recommend reforms that fundamentally redefine the role of legal institutions and procedures in the regulatory process. Yet the OSHA case, which parallels the experiences of other large agencies, leaves responsible policy analysts acutely aware of the shortcomings of the present system and the need for reform.

There is no doubt that the relentlessly formal American regulatory process is unwieldy, inefficient, and expensive, especially by comparison with that of other comparably developed nations. Yet procedural formality does not foster continuity and integrity in administrative decision making. Law, as applied to the resolution of regulatory controversy, seems incapable of preventing capture, but rather operates as just another technique to be manipulated for political gain by those in command of the administrative agencies. There is little evidence that the emphasis on adversarial procedures leads to clearer identification of problems or a balanced appraisal of policy alternatives. Judicial review often occurs too late in the regulatory process to compensate for mistakes, mismanagement, and downright abuses of discretion.

But the costly and time-consuming American approach to rule making serves valuable purposes as well. The processes of formal analysis and open decision making provide the public with incomparably more information about the way their government works than is available to citizens in any other Western country. Substantive issues are explored more systematically and in greater detail. Adversarial procedures permit challenge to established or elitist views, even in areas of technical complexity, and the structured rules of public participation provide access to groups that often are overlooked and excluded in less egalitarian political systems.

The defects of regulatory decision making illustrated by the OSHA case justify the continual experimentation with institutional and procedural forms that is among the most striking characteristics of U.S. policy. It is a sign of vitality in the administrative process that new ideas are developed and implemented in abundant profusion. But the foregoing analysis of OSHA's decision making points to two rather general conclusions that often are overlooked in the discussion of specific reform initiatives. One unavoidable lesson is that the administrative process must develop far greater sensitivity to the social and cultural foundations of science. A better understanding of the nature of uncertainty and the procedures that scientists use to judge the quality of one another's work has to inform the analysis of scientific information by judges and administrators. And administrative procedures must be flexible enough to accommodate the processes used within science to establish quality and legitimacy.

The second point relates to the training of lawyers for public service. If administration is to be left largely in the hands of lawyers, then their education and values become matters of enormous social concern. Unlike the civil servants of other Western countries, American lawyers are not trained to think primarily in terms of the public interest. Their talents are not directed toward the formulation of broad, collective goals, but are available for hire to help achieve policies conceived by clients with narrower political interests. As a result, few lawyers come to government with the credentials needed to inspire public trust, or even the skills required to forge arguments among political adversaries. In the area of social regulation, however, we need a different breed of lawyer, one who is sensitive to the need for compromise, and is neither identified with particular special interests nor driven by an overriding desire for victories in the courtroom. Teaching lawyers in government how to avoid the limiting and destructive polarities of litigation may well be the greatest challenge for American public administration in the next decade.

NOTES

1. Ironically, some of the most penetrating critiques of the adversarial regulatory process have originated with lawyers. See, for example, Peter H. Schuck, "Litigation, Bargaining, and Regulation," *Regulation,* July/August 1979, pp. 26-34.

2. For an extensive comparison of the European and American approaches to legitimating regulatory policy, see Ronald Brickman, Sheila Jasanoff, and Thomas Ilgen, *Controlling Chemicals: The Politics of Regulation in Europe and the U.S.* (Ithaca, NY: Cornell University Press, 1985).

3. See, for example, Joseph L. Badaracco, "A Study of Adversarial and Cooperative Relationships Between Business and Government in Four Countries" (Report prepared for U.S. Department of Commerce, Office of Technology, Strategy and Evaluation, Washington, D.C., 1981); David Vogel, "Cooperative Regulation: Environmental Regulation in Great Britain," *Public Interest* 72 (1983): 88-106; Brickman et al., *Controlling Chemicals,* 1985.

4. Nicholas Ashford, *Crisis in the Workplace: Occupational Disease and Injury* (Cambridge, MA: MIT Press, 1976).

5. See, for example, American Industrial Health Council, "AIHC Proposal for a Science Panel," Scarsdale, NY, March 18, 1980.

6. A classic exposition of this view may be found in Kenneth C. Davis, *Discretionary Justice: A Preliminary Inquiry* (Urbana: University of Illinois Press, 1977). See also Thomas McGarity, "Substantive and Procedural Discretion in Administrative Resolution of Science Policy Questions: Regulating Carcinogens in EPA and OSHA," *Georgetown Law Journal* (1979): 724-810.

7. For a fuller development of this argument, see Sheila Jasanoff, "Science and the Limits of Administrative Rule-Making: Lessons from the OSHA Cancer Policy," *Osgoode Hall Law Journal* 20 (1982): 536-561.

8. Robert Pear, "Congress Moves to Shift Judicial Review Standards," *New York Times,* 4 April 1982.

9. American Petroleum Institute v. Occupational Safety and Health Administration, 581 F.2d 493 (5th Cir., 1978).

10. Industrial Union Department, AFL-CIO v. American Petroleum Institute, 448 U.S. 607 (1980).

11. See, for example, United States v. Lexington Mill and Elevator Co., 232 U.S. 399 (1914); Monsanto v. Kennedy, 613 F.2d 947 (D.C. Cir., 1979).

12. 448 U.S. at 655.

13. "Proposed Firing of Dr. Peter Infante by OSHA: A Case Study in Science and Regulation" (Hearing before the Subcommittee on Investigations and Oversight, Committee on Science and Technology, U.S. House of Representatives, 97th Congress, 1st Session, July 16, 1981), pp. 61-62.

14. Public Citizen Health Research Group v. Auchter, 702 F.2d 1150 (D.C. Cir., 1983).

6

SENSE AND SENTIMENT IN OCCUPATIONAL SAFETY AND HEALTH PROGRAMS

Mark Sagoff

Mobil Oil, Union Carbide, Chrysler, Ford Motor, Thoikol, Anaconda, Bethlehem Steel, Minnesota Mining . . . companies such as these shrug at the pleas of workers whose health they destroy to save money. . . . They ravage the people as they have the land, causing millions to suffer needlessly and hundreds of thousands to die.[1]

Rachel Scott concludes her book, *Muscle and Blood*, with this condemnation of American industry. She continues:

This slaughter is industry's cardinal secret, hidden from public scrutiny beyond plant gates, guarded jealously, supposedly to protect "trade secrets" and for "security reasons." . . . The truth has been hidden so successfully for so long perhaps because if the truth were known, the American profit system would be shaken to its roots.[2]

In the twelve chapters that precede this conclusion, Scott describes in heart-rending detail incidents in which workers, exposed to hazards corporate managers callously refused to change, have been poisoned, crippled, or killed. Scott includes photographs of a few of the victims and even of a victim's

Author's Note: *This chapter is based on work supported by National Science Foundation Grant ISP-81121920*

tombstone. The photographs make all the more poignant the anguish one feels in reading these accounts.

Contrast this approach to that adopted by Martin Bailey in *Reducing Risks to Life: Measurement of the Benefits*, a pamphlet published in 1980 by the American Enterprise Institute. Bailey tells no horror stories about workplace conditions. He includes no pictures of dying workers surrounded by family, friends, and pets. The only illustrations you find in his essay are tables describing, for example, the "Implied Willingness of a Family of Four to Pay for a Health and Safety Program" and the "Dillingham Estimates of the Value of Life."

Scott and Bailey address the same issue, occupational safety and health, but in altogether different terms. Scott appeals to our moral intuitions: Corporate managers, she says, kill workers "to save money." Bailey describes the problem as an economic one. The management of risk in the workplace, he warns, is neither cost-effective nor efficient. The right kind of management, as Bailey sees it, "depends on measuring the costs and benefits of alternative programs and selecting that set of programs and levels of spending that gives the greatest excess of benefits over costs."[3]

Which perspective is better? Should deaths and injuries on the job be viewed as "crimes of greed," as Scott describes them, or as possible "inefficiencies," as Bailey suggests? Are we trying to solve a moral problem or an economic one, or both? What, if any, is the relation between these two approaches to regulation? This chapter will argue that both of these perspectives are needed to inform social policy for occupational safety and health.

ENGAGED AND DETACHED PERSPECTIVES

The ugly incidents Rachel Scott describes move us to anger and pity. The general indictment Scott infers from these incidents—corporations kill workers to increase profits—is, however, contentious. One can argue that a corporation kills "to save money"whenever a death occurs that could have been avoided had the company spent more on safety. Scott's indictment is sometimes accurate; the reason it is contentious is that we have no way to tell when it is not accurate. We have no universally accepted standard or rule by which to determine when a workplace is safe enough, when, for example, an injury or death is not to be described as a "crime of greed."

Workers will suffer and die as a result of workplace hazards even when corporations go to great lengths to protect them, for example, by installing expensive pollution control equipment, as the companies Scott mentions generally have done. As Scott provides no criterion for telling how safe is safe enough, we do not know how far to generalize the conclusion she draws from a selection of staggering examples. Do corporations as a rule "shrug at the pleas of workers whose health they destroy to save money?" Do companies, in general, strive to meet an adequate standard for workplace safety instead?

How much should industry spend to protect worker safety and health? That this question has no plain or intuitive answer becomes obvious when one considers, as Bailey does, the costs companies must bear to comply with particular regulations. In 1977, for example, the Occupational Safety and Health Administration (OSHA) proposed to reduce from 10 to 1 part per million (ppm) the permissible ambient exposure level for benzene, a carcinogen for which no safe threshold level is known and which is used in a wide range of industrial processes. The American Petroleum Institute promptly challenged the standard in court contending, among other things, that no study had shown a significant connection between benzene and cancer at exposure levels below 25 ppm. Lawyers for industry argued, moreover, that the benefits of the new standard would be negligible: The difference in risk to any worker would be so small—indeed, insignificant—that it could not justify the required investment of hundreds of millions of dollars in new equipment. The U.S. Court of Appeals for the

Fifth Circuit agreed with the American Petroleum Institute and invalidated the 1 ppm standard.[4] The Supreme Court, in a 1980 decision deeply divided along many lines, affirmed the Appeals Court decision and remanded the standard back to OSHA for revision.[5]

How shall we evaluate the outcome of this case? It is altogether possible that a small number of workers, let us suppose about a dozen, could get cancer at the 10 ppm level who would not under the 1 ppm standard. Shall we accuse the plurality of justices, then, of conspiring with industrialists who kill to save money? Shall we take the opposite view, namely, that the Supreme Court drew a line against ideologues in OSHA who were intent on bankrupting American corporations? A middle position also is possible. We might say that the court made a decision in a case so complex and difficult that it admitted of no clearly right resolution. We might not expect the courts to act with the wisdom of Solomon in resolving issues so difficult that our own moral intuitions, when we ponder the same questions, boggle and break down.

In order to understand the relation of our moral intuitions to complex regulatory problems and policies, we may distinguish between what we may call (following Allan Gibbard)[6] engaged and detached styles of decision making. This distinction is well illustrated, for example, in a passage in *The Methods of Ethics*, in which Henry Sidgwick discusses "any game which involves—as most games do—a contest for victory."[7] A player as he or she enters into a game may do so simply from a desire to play; he or she will not seek victory as much as "the pleasant struggle for it."[8] This changes as soon as the game begins, for once the player is engaged in the sport, "a transient desire to win the game is generally indispensable."[9]

The contrast Sidgwick draws between our engaged and detached attitudes toward competitive games applies as well to our social decisions regarding safety and health. Heroic efforts to rescue people trapped in mines or lost at sea, for example, or to save children afflicted by disease may cost large sums that could save many more lives if used, for example, for driver education or school lunch programs. Those engaged in rescue attempts, however, have in mind the plight of a particular group of miners or the life of a particular child. The fact that their efforts and resources might be spent more "effectively" or more "efficiently" if invested, for example, in safety equipment or in teaching hygiene makes no difference to them. They simply see what the immediate situation—a miner is trapped, a child needs blood—demands of them.

The examples of exploitation Rachel Scott describes share an important characteristic with stories about heroic rescues, heinous crimes, and other fortunes and misfortunes that inspire sympathy or arouse indignation. These situations present a moral landscape that is open to immediate view; we look and see what is to be done. No strange complexities hide the path; no second thoughts or mitigating circumstances puzzle the will.

The situation changes dramatically when we come to consider not isolated actions but general policies, for example, for safety aboard ships and in mines, for preventing and prosecuting crimes, for relieving suffering, and for helping those in need. We must now balance opposing interests and weigh conflicting intuitions. We now may speak not of particular but of statistical lives; we think in terms not of death but of the risk of death. And we make policy decisions that may result in fatalities that, were we confronted with them, we should go to spectacular lengths to prevent. The miner will suffocate and the child will drown, in part because we were unwilling to spend, perhaps, just a few more cents on safety for every miner or every swimmer. Our considered social policy, then, may lead to results completely different from those we would seek to achieve on the basis of immediate sympathies and moral intuitions.

Are we, then, hypocritical? Do we kill miners, children, and animals "to save money" while knocking ourselves out for the occasional individual whom we can see and who thus tugs at

our conscience? Is the tennis player hypocritical whose objective is winning only when he or she is engaged in playing the
game? The "detached" perspective of policy analysis will
produce results, no doubt, that we might regret the moment
our intuitions are engaged in contemplating them in the plight
of particular individuals. This regret may suggest that the
detached perspective is inhuman or, perhaps, that the engaged
perspective is sentimental. It seems we cannot do without
either perspective; yet, if they are inconsistent, we cannot
always act upon both.

WILLINGNESS TO PAY

Martin Bailey proposes, as a criterion for social policies and
decisions, the principle of economic efficiency or, as he says,
the rule that for any policy "the benefits to whomsoever they
accrue exceed the costs."[10] The costs of a program are measured in terms of the resources society must commit and the
opportunities it must forgo to have that program. The benefits
"are measured by the amount the beneficiaries would be
willing to pay for the goods and services provided by the
program."[11] Efficient resource management, Bailey advises,
depends on selecting the programs that give the greatest excess
of benefits over costs. The goal of resource management, in
other words, is to give people more of what they are willing to
pay for, that is, more of what they happen to want to buy.

In order to judge the effectiveness and the efficiency of
government programs in the area of health and safety, as
Bailey argues, we need to determine some figure X "to
represent the total amount of benefits enjoyed by all the
population whose risk is reduced, scaled for convenience in
units of lives saved."[12] Bailey considers government programs
intended to reduce risk and save lives to be justified only if

these programs cost, as a rule, no more than X per life saved. "Failure to use an explicit value X to help determine the resource limit for each program inevitably lowers the efficiency of the entire set of programs."[13]

Bailey contends that there is no rational case to be made for public programs that require us to spend "a huge sum to avoid a death from one cause while refusing to spend a relatively small sum to avoid a death from another cause."[14] Nevertheless, as rational, well-informed individuals "do not equalize these incremental sums precisely in private choices . . . a policy based on these choices will allow some, albeit minor, differences in these sums to remain."[15]

Bailey discusses a number of ways to determine X or the value of a program per life saved, including approaches that base this value on one's earning potential or on one's contribution to the gross national product. He prefers an approach based on the willingness of people to pay for their own safety, the most direct evidence for which, he writes, "comes from the job market, which offers a variety of working environments with various degrees of personal risk."[16] Workers generally demand more money to do riskier work. "For such workers, the wage differential precisely measures their willingness to pay for increased safety."[17]

The "value per life saved" may be inferred as well from other evidence, for example, from life insurance premiums and markets for safety devices. Bailey reviews some of the studies that have "shed light on the approximate willingness to pay for safety in the United States"[18] and that have offered estimates concerning the value of each life saved. Bailey recommends that government agencies use some such value, derived by experts from meticulous empirical studies of willingness to pay, to make policy for consumer product safety and for occupational safety and health.

In order to evaluate Bailey's recommendation, we should ask why, if efficiency is his goal, he would permit government intervention into private transactions at all, even interventions based on some conception of average willingness to pay. One might have thought that levels of safety should be determined "at the margin" through voluntary informed transactions between workers and employers or between producers and consumers, on the basis of what each individual believes is beneficial or acceptable to him or her. Workers then would be free to choose unsafe conditions, for example, in exchange for a higher wage or for discounts at the company store; consumers who prefer more goods to safer goods, moreover, would be free to make that choice. As long as individuals can buy the safety they are willing to pay for—as long as they are not inhibited, for example, by free-rider problems, bargaining inequalities, and transaction costs—why should we need anything more? We may assume that whatever safety levels result from transactions of this kind will be socially efficient.

Now, we simply must recognize that consumers often do prefer more goods to safer goods; the market for cigarettes confirms this. Warning labels are there, but smokers ignore them. Vast numbers of horrible deaths occur as a result. Workers, too, have died in droves on the job not necessarily because they were prevented from trading safety for higher wages but precisely because they were permitted to do so. The money looks good "up front"; the deaths and injuries are hypothetical and come after a while. Accordingly, health and safety had become "back burner" issues in many collective bargaining agreements before OSHA. Jack Suarez, then health and safety director for the International Union of Engineers, put the matter as follows. "In negotiating a contract, it appears that health and safety clauses come after coffee breaks."[19]

One may wonder, then, why Bailey believes the government should intervene at all; why, for example, there should be OSHA regulations. We can put the question this way: Either markets for safety are efficient or they are not. If they are efficient, from the point of view of economic theory, there is no reason for the government to intervene in them. But if they are not efficient, they are unlikely to provide the information we need to determine worker willingness to pay for health and safety and, thus, to make them more efficient. The dilemma is particularly jarring, indeed, because people are willing to pay more to protect themselves from some risks than others. Accordingly, it seems arbitrary to apply in uranium mines, let us say, a value per life saved derived from markets for safety glass.

Bailey concedes the general efficiency of labor markets when he writes that the "most direct evidence of the amount people are willing to pay for their own safety comes from the job market."[20] If the job market functions well enough to reveal what workers are willing to pay for safety, it must function well enough to give them the safety for which they are willing to pay. This is true, incidentally, even if workers trade safety for coffee breaks. As long as they trade voluntarily and with enough information, the exchange is cost-beneficial, at least from Bailey's point of view. If the transaction is informed and voluntary, it simply does not matter how many deaths and injuries result. Bailey might wish the government to inform workers about the risks they take in order to make sure that they consent to work under hazardous conditions. Beyond that, how does he justify government regulations at all—even regulations based, for instance, on the Dillingham estimates of the value of life?

I believe that Rachel Scott understands better than Martin Bailey the reason that we regulate safety in the workplace, in consumer products, and in the environment. The reason is not to make markets efficient, to internalize externalities, or to maximize benefits over costs. These latter concepts are academic; they appeal to people who have graduate school degrees; they have the stink of the lamp about them. The reason we regulate, rather, is to minimize sickness, injury, and death. Misery and death are bad things, terrible things, and Americans collectively, through government, have a *prima facie* right—indeed, an obligation—to do something about

them when they mount up, whether they result from transactions in efficient markets or not.

COARSE-GRAINED AND FINE-GRAINED POLICIES

The need for laws to govern the workplace is obvious. These
laws are enacted to prevent the suffering, misery, and exploitation likely to occur without them. Earlier this century,
legislatures passed minimum wage and maximum hour laws
in response to the worst abuses associated with sweatshops and
company towns. The picture of children sweltering ten or
twelve hours a day in sordid textile mills simply is abhorrent to
and impossible within a civilized society, and this is all that
need be and should be said in defense of child labor laws. No
economic and no free market argument is needed to show that
children should be raised and educated and not sent to tend
bobbins when they are eight. Likewise, no one but a moral idiot
would require a cost-benefit analysis before the government
intervenes in an industry in which the cancer rate is 5 or 10%.
    Although it is obvious that benzene levels of 50 or 100 ppm
in the workplace are too high (the resulting body count would
be unacceptable on moral grounds), we do not know what to
say about levels under 20 ppm. At these levels the evidence of
danger is scanty or nonexistent. The costs of lowering standards increase dramatically, moreover, as the permitted levels
of exposure become increasingly small. Our moral intuitions
and human sympathies, however engaged by accounts of gross
negligence, are indecisive when hazards are small and the costs
of reducing them are great.
    At this fine-grained level of policy making the "detached"
techniques of risk-benefit analysis are most useful. These
techniques encourage partisans on either side of a tough policy
question to focus attention on a range of issues, often technical,
that can be argued intelligently by those having a degree of

expertise. These issues include the appropriate value X per life saved, the "pricing" of externalities, and other problems attending the measurement of benefits and costs.

When a controversy is carried on in cost-benefit terms, partisans will argue, moreover, about theoretical matters as far afield as the analysis of epidemiological data and the social discount rate. On these issues an immense literature exists and an even more immense literature waits to be written. Academic papers will appear; college curricula will be prepared; concerned and vocal individuals, who might otherwise become disgruntled, will hire themselves out as experts and collect fees and grants. It may not matter much at the end of this process (if it ever ends) what the decision is, indeed, even if there is a decision; it may not matter much, for example, if OSHA lowers the benzene standard to 1 ppm from 10. By the time such a decision wends its way through the political process and the courts, a new administration may reverse it anyway, or a new technology, introduced for extraneous reasons, will alter completely the risks to safety and health.

EFFICIENCY OR EMPATHY?

What are the alternatives to risk-benefit analysis? Two are all that come to mind: First, we may appeal to ethical sentiments and moral intuitions; second, we may attempt to infer a decision from the language and intent of Congress. Our ethical sentiments, when engaged, help us to make large-scale decisions; they tell us to eliminate, for example, gross horrors and abuses of the sort Rachel Scott presents. These intuitions become confused and uncertain, however, when they confront fine-grained decisions: for example, tradeoffs between minute reductions of risk and mounting compliance costs. To debate tradeoffs of this sort in the language of morality—to debate, in other words, what justice, sympathy, and mutual respect demand—is to invite impasse, as morality does not speak with a single voice in these decisions and we may be justified as a nation to make them either way.

Similarly, legislative language and intent are likely to be as vague as our moral intuitions and for many of the same reasons. Accordingly, policy makers often are compelled, *faute de mieux*, to use risk-benefit analysis to make close calls among proposed rules or standards that pass ethical and legal muster. The question of whether a standard passes ethical and legal muster, of course, must be settled on ethical and legal grounds: It cannot be decided by cost-benefit analysis. Nevertheless, the detached economic perspective Bailey recommends may become relevant, even dispositive, when we choose between alternative regulations, each of which meets legal and moral tests.

Notions of economic efficiency may be relevant to regulatory policy, then, even though efficiency is not the reason for or the purpose of regulation. The reason that we regulate risk is to achieve broadly utilitarian and humanitarian ends. We recognize that markets, however efficient, will not always achieve those ends. On the contrary, as history shows, free market transactions may just as easily lead to misery and grief. Fortunately, we have political freedom to act upon our engaged human sympathies and values and thus freedom to spare ourselves by prohibiting horrors of the kind we might suffer as consumers or workers as a result of market decisions. We use our political freedom—a freedom well circumscribed by a bill of individual rights—to limit what would otherwise be a dangerous because uncircumscribed freedom of markets.

Economists who believe, as Bailey might, that efficiency rather than love or sympathy is the reason for regulation have a problem. They must reconcile their empathetic and civilized instincts (their engaged intuitions) with policies justified simply on detached cost-benefit grounds. They may do this easily enough, of course, by telling "just so" stories to "show" that regulations required for moral reasons really are necessary to "internalize" externalities and minimize transaction costs.

As market failures exist in the eye of the beholder, these stories are easy to tell. One may tautologously reconcile ethical and economic perspectives on policy making also by shadow pricing "moralisms," "fragile values," and "equity benefits." When one does this "correctly," one can easily and quickly justify on grounds of economic sense any policy that appeals to moral sentiment.

The reason economists engage in this sort of story telling and shadow pricing is sometimes to save their own theory from embarrassing consequences; it cannot always be to give insight into public policy. So be it. Economists generally are a gentle crew and they wish to endorse the regulatory and environmental policies that our engaged moral intuitions and sympathies demand. Many economists feel comfortable, however, only when they have discovered a market failure, a free-rider problem, a competitive dilemma, or something by which they can justify morally sound policies on detached theoretical grounds.

At the end of the last century, the Supreme Court reviewed a variety of state laws regulating the workplace. In its decisions, the Supreme Court emphasized that restricting the freedom to contract for personal employment was a "substantial impairment of liberty" that was "as essential to the laborer as to the capitalist, to the poor as to the rich."[21] The court in 1897 reviewed a state law extending protection to miners and upheld it on the ground that miners constituted a sort of captive labor force that could not bargain equitably with its employers.[22] In Lochner v. New York (1905),[23] however, the court found bakers to be in an equitable bargaining position and saw no reason, therefore, that the state should interfere with their freedom to make whatever contracts they wished. Accordingly, the Lochner court invalidated a state law setting a 10-hour daily and a 60-hour weekly maximum for employment of bakers.

Many theorists today defend the general principle laid down in these cases, namely, that the state may interfere in a free market contract only to redress a bargaining inequality or correct a market failure, but not on other ethical or humanitarian grounds. This principle is easy to maintain in the face of counter-examples, for one can always tell a story to "show" that whatever intervention morality or compassion requires really is necessary to redress a bargaining inequality or to correct a market inefficiency. A review of tort litigation with respect to consumer products and workplace safety suggests, however, that juries are moved by a sense of public decency, compassion, and outrage in determining awards in these cases.[24]

Health and safety legislation—OSHA is only one example—express our engaged values and sentiments: a sense of compassion, mutual responsibility, and reverence for life. Americans are a compassionate and caring people and that is why we are not going back to the terrible conditions of a century ago—no matter what fully informed individuals may do in equitable and efficient markets. We do not need to tell an "equity" or an "efficiency" story to justify our compassionate and often paternalistic laws; we need only point out how much death and mayhem they prevent. Needless to say, theorists can always find reasons to believe that statutory and common laws address bargaining inequalities and inefficiencies; but this helps us to defend an academic theory rather than to understand these laws.

Nevertheless, we also confront the law of diminishing returns. At some point we must rely on a detached attitude to decide when to allow workers and employers to come to their own terms regarding marginal increases or decreases in workplace safety. Here we may well be guided by detached or theoretical attitudes and we may discuss equity and efficiency in workplace contracts. The basic justification for occupational and consumer health and safety regulations, nevertheless, lies in a sense of what a civilized society may and may not tolerate. One does not need graduate courses in philosophy and economics to understand that shocking conditions prior to 1970 amply justified the major provisions of OSHA.

MARKETS OR MORALS?

Bailey, in a rhetorical passage, says that the basic question at issue concerns the function of government: "Should the government provide services people want" or "the services experts believe people need, whether they want them or not?"[25] How does Bailey stand on this question? Consider, for example, a group of macho workers who, though informed of the risks, would agree to work under egregiously unsafe conditions because "it won't happen to them." Consider impoverished workers who must take these jobs or none. Consider, moreover, consumers who, to save a few dollars, would buy an unsafe hair dryer or microwave, in spite of the printed warnings. Bailey may believe (and properly so) that these individuals should not make the transactions they are willing to make but the transactions risk-benefit analysts in government think they should make instead. Bailey, in any event, apparently would allow these experts to require that workplace conditions or consumer products come up to decent safety standards—call them "risk-beneficial" standards, if you like—and that safety levels therefore should be determined politically and should not be left to the market.

The efficiency strategy Bailey favors looks like a market strategy, to be sure, because it is based on market data; these data, however, are not anything like the data these same markets would have provided 50 or 100 years ago. Rather, the studies Bailey cites are based on market behavior conditioned by a century of paternalistic and humanitarian regulation. Bailey's cost-benefit approach is conservative because it retains for the future, as cost-benefit thinking tends to do, prices paid for things in the past; but it also retains, ironically, a century of liberal reforms that are reflected in those prices. It is hard to justify without circularity our public decisions regarding safety on the basis of our private ones, as the latter are conditioned by a history of regulation based on public discussion and political action. This kind of circularity, however, may be benign. To mix the metaphor: Bailey uses the rhetoric of efficiency as a smokescreen to hide regulations that are based on public morality rather than on private interest. It is easier for some people to accept such regulations when they are presented with that kind of disguise.

At this point it must occur to us to think that Martin Bailey, like Rachel Scott, would be appalled by and would want to prohibit incidents of the sort Scott describes—even if these result from voluntary, informed, and uncoerced market transactions with no costs to third parties. The reason that Bailey would allow the government to step in to prevent voluntary transactions of a gruesome sort—transactions in which people risk too much for the sake of too little—might have to do with common human decency and not with anything in his economic theory. Bailey, in other words, is not necessarily a libertarian or a free market ideologue who would accept as morally satisfying the outcome of *any* voluntary informed transaction, even duelling, heroin consumption, and so on, however high the body count may be. Rather, he may, like the rest of us, want to lower the body count not simply to make markets efficient but as a matter of common decency and societal self-respect.

CONCLUSION

Rachel Scott reminds us that the source of our concern with occupational safety and health—the basic reason for it—has nothing directly to do with efficiency. It has no logical or conceptual relation to cost-benefit analysis. The basis of our concern, rather, lies in our moral intuitions; it also is found in our pride, dignity, and sense of national responsibility. It does not matter to us whether incidents of the sort Scott describes arise in perfect or in imperfect markets. One could tell a story to show that these episodes are examples of efficiency and a

story to show that they are not. That is beside the point. The
point is that these incidents are morally outrageous; common
decency, not market analysis, impels us to prohibit them.

We may agree whole-heartedly with Scott, however, and still
appreciate the value of many of Bailey's suggestions. Bailey
appeals to market principles, to be sure, in order to justify what
are, in fact, governmental interventions. This appeal, we hope,
amounts to little more than a rhetorical flourish, as no caring
humane person would allow the market—even a perfect
market—to determine standards for occupational safety and
health. Death on the job cries up to heaven and we must
prevent it whether by conjuring up tables of "average willingness to pay" or by publishing pictures of dying workers and
their pet dogs. We should not be bogged down in these
differences in rhetoric and style; we cannot substitute analysis
for action. We agree as a society that death, illness, and misery
on the job are bad things and that we as a society are obligated
to use the power of the law to minimize them.

Social guilt and a conception of social solidarity, not a desire
to make markets efficient, lie behind and justify our collective
political decisions regarding risk in the workplace. This is as it
should be and, indeed, as it must be in a society that is
concerned about its character, its quality, and its traditions. It
is hard to talk about social guilt and pride, however; it is even
harder to base tough policy choices on these "engaged" moral
intuitions. And it may be harder still to admit that we are acting
sometimes as our brothers' keepers to protect individuals not
only from another but also, paternalistically, from themselves.

Public officials in regulatory agencies cover their embar-
rassment behind a smokescreen of professionalism by adopting the "detached" style of policy making. They prefer cost-
benefit analysis to the sometimes evangelical terms of engaged
social criticism. These officials then justify their decisions on
"value-free," "neutral," and "scientific" and not on "emotional" or "sentimental" grounds. This is one reason policy
makers prefer to speak in terms of the benefit value X per life
saved rather than in terms of the social guilt Y per life lost.

The value X may reflect the guilt Y, however, if the policy maker uses the "right" market data (as Bailey does) or gives equity "costs" the "right" shadow price. The moral intuitions that the "scientific" policy maker throws out the front door of his or her analysis promptly reenter by the back. This makes sense: It is the genius of our system. We use the detached rhetoric of economic sense to explain policies that we require on the basis of engaged ethical sentiment.

NOTES

1. Rachel Scott, *Muscle and Blood* (New York: Dutton, 1974), pp. 292-293.

2. Ibid., p. 293.

3. Martin Bailey, *Reducing Risks to Life: A Measurement of the Benefits* (Washington, DC: American Enterprise Institute, 1980), p. 2. All references to Bailey are to this book.

4. American Petroleum Institute v. Marshall, 581 F. 2d 493 (5th Cir. 1978).

5. 448 U.S. 607 (1980).

6. Allen Gibbard, "Risk and Value," in *Values at Risk*, ed. Douglas MacLean (Totowa, NJ: Rowman and Allenheld, in press).

7. Henry Sidgwick, *The Methods of Ethics* (London: MacMillan, 1907), Bk. II, Ch. III, Sec. 2, p. 135f.

8. Ibid.

9. Ibid.

10. Bailey, p. 15 (quoting the Flood Control Act of 1936).

11. Ibid., p. 17.

12. Ibid., p. 19.

13. Ibid., p. 49.

14. Ibid., p. 10.

15. Ibid., p. 10.

16. Ibid., p. 31.

17. Ibid., p. 31.

18. Ibid., p. 35.

19. Bureau of National Affairs, *OSHA and the Unions: Bargaining on Job Safety and Health* (Washington, DC: BNA, 1977).

20. Bailey, p. 31.

21. Coppage v. Kansas 236 U.S. 1 at 14.

22. Holden v. Hardy 166 U.S. 366, 393, 397 (1897).

23. 198 U.S. 45 (1905). Justice Peckman wrote for the court (at 57): "There is no contention that bakers as a class are not equal in intelligence and capacity to men in other trades or manual occupations, or that they are not able to assert their rights and care for themselves without the protecting arm of the state, interfering with their independence of judgment and action."

24. See George Eads and Peter Reuter, *Designing Safer Products: Corporate Responses to Product Liability Law and Regulation* (Santa Monica, CA: Rand, 1983), esp. Sec. II.

25. Bailey, p. 21.

ABOUT THE CONTRIBUTORS

MICHAEL S. BROWN is Research Associate in the Center for the Study of Drug Development at Tufts University Medical School. He is coauthor with Dorothy Nelkin of *Workers at Risk: Voices From the Workplace* (University of Chicago Press, 1984).

STEPHEN HILGARTNER is a Ph.D. student in the Department of Sociology at Cornell University. He is coauthor of *Nukespeak: The Selling of Nuclear Technology in America* (Sierra Books and Penguin, 1982).

SHEILA JASANOFF is Associate Professor in the Cornell University Program on Science, Technology, and Society. A lawyer specializing in regulatory policy, she is coauthor of *Chemical Controls: Regulating Politics in Europe and the United States* (Cornell University Press, 1984).

DOROTHY NELKIN is Professor in the Program on Science, Technology, and Society and the Department of Sociology at Cornell University. She is the author of numerous books, including *Controversy* (Sage Publications, 1984); *The Creation Controversy* (Beacon Press, 1984); and coauthor with Michael Brown of *Workers at Risk* (University of Chicago Press, 1984).

CHRIS ANNE RAYMOND is a sociologist specializing in communications. She is a project researcher at the Museum of Science and Industry in Chicago.

MARK SAGOFF is a philosopher in the Program on Philosophy and Public Affairs at the University of Maryland.